C000256746

Phonics and Spelling

Ages 8–9

Julie Crimmins-Crocker

Published by Collins
An imprint of HarperCollins*Publishers*
77–85 Fulham Palace Road
Hammersmith
London
W6 8JB

Browse the complete Collins catalogue at
www.collinseducation.com

© HarperCollins*Publishers* Limited 2011, on behalf of the author
First published in 2007 by Folens Limited.

ISBN-13: 978-0-00-745238-5

Julie Crimmins-Crocker asserts her moral right to be identified as the author of this work.

British Library Cataloguing in Publication Data
A catalogue record for this publication is available from the British Library.

Every effort has been made to trace copyright holders and to obtain their permission for the use of copyright material. The authors and publishers will gladly receive any information enabling them to rectify any error or omission in subsequent editions.

Managing editor: Joanne Mitchell
Editor: Melody Ismail
Layout artist: Neil Hawkins, ndesign
Illustrations: Helen Jackson and Nicola Pearce of SGA and Leonie Shearing c/o Lucas Alexander Whitley.
Cover design for this edition: Julie Martin
Design and layout for this edition: Linda Miles, Lodestone Publishing
Printed and bound in China.

Contents

This contents list provides an overview of the learning objectives of each puzzle page.

How to complete the puzzles

 Read the title and the instructions for each activity very carefully.

 For each activity, start with the simplest clues first.

Crossword and wordsearch clues have numbers at the end of each clue to tell you how many letters there are in the word.

 If there is a word bank for you to refer to, check that your answers are in the list. Cross out the words in the word bank as you complete the clue.

 Use a sharp pencil at first to write down all your answers (just in case you need to change them).

 When you are sure your answers are correct, write them in pen or use a highlighter pen for the wordsearches.

 In the crosswords, write in CAPITAL LETTERS. This will make your answers easier to read.

Use a dictionary and thesaurus to help you spell and find your answers.

After each puzzle go to 'What's next' (page 5) and cross off the completed activity.

Remember what these useful words mean:

Synonym: the same or similar meaning, for example, *big – large*.

Antonym: the opposite meaning, for example, *big – small*.

Anagram: the word is muddled up, for example, *GREAL – LARGE*.

Informal: the word is simple or slang, for example, *rabbit – bunny*.

Verbs are action and 'doing' words, for example, *run*, *talk* and *think*.

Nouns are naming words, for example, *pen*, *hat*, *apple* and *school*.

Adjectives are describing words, for example, *small* bird.

Adverbs add more information to verbs, for example, *He ran **quickly***.

Phoneme: a letter or letters that create a single sound when said aloud, for example, **TH** and **OO**.

Letter string: a collection of phonemes, for example, **ELL**.

Vowels are the letters **a**, **e**, **i**, **o** and **u**.

Consonants are the letters of the alphabet which are <u>not</u> vowels.

What's next?

Use the answers to any of the puzzles to complete the following activities. Write down which activity you have completed and the date you did it.

	Activity	Puzzle title	Date
1	Sort the answers into **alphabetical order**. Put them in a list.		
2	Put the answers into **sentences** (10 sentences minimum). You can use one word per sentence or include as many words as you like in each sentence.		
3	Put the answers into sentences that are questions. For example, *Where did my cat go?*		
4	Put the answers into sentences that are instructions. For example, *Look after my cat when I am away.*		
5	Put the words in the word bank into a story or piece of writing.		
6	Write at least ten more of the same type of word.		
7	Find **synonyms** for the words and write them down in pairs or groups. For example, *big – large, massive.*		
8	Find **antonyms** for the words and write them down in pairs or groups. For example, *big – small, tiny, minute.*		
9	Find **rhymes** for the words and list them. For example, *ink – sink* and *bellow – yellow, mellow* and *fellow.*		
10	Sort the answers into groups. For example, verbs, nouns, adjectives, adverbs, number of syllables, rhyming words and so on.		
11	Write your own new clues for the answers to a crossword, wordsearch or puzzle or create a totally new puzzle.		

Medium frequency words

Add the missing words below to show the **present tense** and **past tense** of each verb. The first one has been done for you.

Verb – present tense	Verb – past tense		Verb – present tense	Verb – past tense
ASK	Asked		OPEN	
BEGIN				SHOWED
	HEARD		THINK	
	KNEW			WATCHED
BRING			WAKE	
	WROTE			USED
START			LEAVE	
FIND			TURN	
	CHANGED		TELL	
JUMP				WALKED

Put the following words in alphabetical order. First, look at the initial letter of each word and then at the second and third letters of each word.

WHERE   PLACE   ANY
BEING   MUCH   NEVER   STILL
UPON   WHILE   WITHOUT
DOES   CHANGE   DON'T
GONE   EVERY   MIGHT   TOLD
TRIES   ONLY   NUMBER

Medium frequency words

Write the answers next to the clues in lower case letters. Then, complete the crossword using upper case letters.

ACROSS
1. One of two equal parts (4)
4. An antonym for over (5)
6. An antonym for after (6)
8. An antonym for last (5)
12. An antonym for inside (7)
15. At all times, forever (6)
18. An antonym for below (5)
20. am not pm (7)
21. Occasionally (9)
22. An antonym for old (5)

DOWN
2. As well, too (4)
3. An antonym for far (4)
5. An antonym for day (5)
7. An antonym for leading (9)
9. Now, not yesterday or tomorrow (5)
10. An antonym for apart (8)
11. Underneath (5)
13. Twelve months (4)
14. Almost (6)
16. The place between first and third (6)
17. Frequently (5)
19. An antonym for low (4)

Simple nouns

Nouns are naming words; they say what things are called. They can be **singular** – *pen*, *bat* and *car* or **plural** – *pens*, *bats* and *cars*.

The answers in this crossword are all nouns. Some are **singular nouns** and some are **plural nouns**.

Word bank

TEACHER	BOXES
TIME	BOOKS
TAIL	EARS
PEOPLE	TRUCK
MEN	MILK
SHEEP	LAMB
PETS	FARM
FISH	FLY
SCHOOL	BABY
DOORS	TOY
DOG	TEA
LEG	BOAT

ACROSS

2. This is measured in hours, minutes and seconds (4)   **4.** More than one man (3)

5. They give us wool (5)   **6.** An insect with wings (3)   **8.** These are tame animals, like dogs or cats (4)   **10.** These are made of cardboard and used to store things in (5)

12. A baby sheep (4)   **14.** You can catch one with a hook and a line (4)   **15.** A builder often drives one (5)   **16.** You open these to get in to places (5)   **17.** Something a child can play with (3)   **18.** A body part with a foot and a knee (3)   **19.** You can sit in it and it floats (4)

DOWN

1. The instructor of the class (7)   **2.** A dog can wag this (4)   **3.** More than one person (6)

6. A place you might find cows and sheep (4)   **7.** It is white and you can drink it (4)

9. Where children go to learn (6)   **10.** They contain lots of pages to read (5)   **11.** You hear with these (4)   **13.** A very young child (4)   **16.** An animal that likes to chase cats (3)

17. A light afternoon meal or a hot drink (3)

Words with EN

EN has a short E phoneme and it can be found in many words, for example, *penguin, men, garden* and *pencil*. EN is also a suffix. It can be added to adjectives to make them into verbs, for example, *I am using **dark** paint* (adjective). *I am going to **darken** the paint* (verb). EN can also be added to verbs when they change tense, for example, *I **woke**; I was **woken** up*.

Using the clues, highlight the words with EN in this wordsearch.

R	T	G	M	R	P	E	N	C	I	L	H	E	N
C	W	O	M	E	N	L	M	E	K	T	N	L	N
K	F	O	B	J	T	L	V	T	N	D	K	E	N
E	A	V	M	K	M	E	L	E	J	T	H	Z	G
N	S	E	W	Z	X	E	N	N	L	C	E	Z	E
V	T	N	T	H	J	P	N	N	T	K	B	R	N
E	E	O	B	D	E	G	E	I	I	N	R	M	T
L	N	F	R	L	V	N	K	N	E	S	Y	X	L
O	F	T	I	O	P	E	N	K	E	T	W	E	E
P	A	E	G	X	Y	Q	C	N	L	R	N	Y	R
E	L	N	H	V	F	I	E	A	M	I	G	P	P
Q	L	T	T	X	U	D	N	G	G	T	B	Y	M
D	E	G	E	Q	R	E	D	N	E	R	N	G	W
T	N	X	N	J	P	J	E	M	E	N	E	M	Y

Word bank

PENCIL	ENERGY
KITCHEN	TENNIS
OFTEN	WOMEN
WHEN	BRIGHTEN
DEN	ENVELOPE
TEN	FALLEN
PENALTY	ENTER
ENGINE	ENEMY
GENTLE	FASTEN
HEN	MEN
QUICKEN	OVEN

1. A room used for cooking (7)   **2.** This word means 'at what time?' (4)   **3.** An antonym for rarely (5)   **4.** A small room or a wild beast's lair (3)   **5.** You use this to draw with (6)   **6.** We eat food to give us the _ _ _ _ _ _ to do things (6)   **7.** Mild not rough (6)   **8.** A free shot at goal awarded for a serious foul near the goal (7)   **9.** A farm bird that lays eggs (3)   **10.** A game with a net, rackets and balls (6)   **11.** 5 + 5 (3)   **12.** Another word for a motor (6)   **13.** The plural of woman (5)   **14.** A cover for a letter (8)   **15.** To attach, fix or secure (6)   **16.** An antonym for exit (5)   **17.** To make lighter (8)   **18.** An antonym for 'to slow down' (7)   **19.** An opponent not a friend (5)   **20.** The plural of man (3)   **21.** An antonym for risen (6)   **22.** A stove or cooker (4)

Find and circle the eight EN words in this letter puzzle.

chick   engen   eral   en   joyth   entent   spendple   ntygen   erous

Words with AN

AN has a short **A** phoneme and it can be found in many words, for example, *panic, banish, anaconda, Japan.* When **ED**, **ER** and **ING** are added to one-syllable words with **AN**, the final **N** is doubled to keep the **A** phoneme short, for example, *plan – planned, planning, planner.*

Sort these words into groups according to the number of syllables in each word.

 ran   banana   tan   planets   fan   Canada   Dan   human
can   animals   plan   caravan   man   began   flan   van
Nan   woman   manager   anagram

1 syllable	2 syllables	3 syllables

Words with AN

Read the clues and write the answers with **AN** in the crossword.

Word bank

TAN	ANAGRAM
VAN	MAN
FLAN	CARAVAN
PLAN	MANAGER
BEGAN	CAN
ANIMALS	DAN
HUMAN	PLANETS
WOMAN	FAN
BANANA	NAN
CANADA	RAN

ACROSS

5. A word with muddled letters that can make a new word (7)
9. A holiday home on wheels that can be towed by a car (7)
10. The country north of the USA (6)
11. A man's name (3)
12. An antonym for woman (3)
13. A vehicle for carrying goods (3)
14. These are found in space and Mars is one of them (7)
16. Another name for a pie or tart (4)
17. Another word for gran (3)

DOWN

1. An antonym for man (5)
2. The past tense of begin (5)
3. A type of animal like you and me (5)
4. A yellow fruit with a thick skin (6)
6. These can be found in a zoo (7)
7. The past tense of run (3)
8. The person in charge (7)
10. A tin container for food or drink (3)
14. Another word for a map (4)
15. Caused by the sun which makes your skin brown (3)
16. This moves the air to cool you down (3)

Words with AP

The letter string **AP** has a short **A** phoneme and it can be found in many words, for example, *clap*, *unwrap* and *kneecap*. When **Y**, **ED**, **ER** and **ING** are added to one-syllable words with **AP**, the final **P** is doubled to keep the **A** phoneme short, for example, *flap – flapped*, *flapper*, *flapping* and *gap – gappy*.

Write the **AP** answers to these clues.

1	A section of a book.	
2	A hat with a peak not a brim.	
3	To fall down and crumple.	
4	To cover with paper.	
5	Another word for a man.	
6	Overturned accidentally in the water (as a boat might be).	
7	The liquid in the stem of plants.	
8	The commander of a ship or the leader of a company of soldiers.	
9	A thin strip possibly of leather.	
10	A plan or flat drawing of an area.	
11	Glad or cheerful.	
12	To turn liquid into vapour so that it dries up.	
13	A country famous for kimonos and sushi.	
14	Water comes out of it.	
15	A short sleep.	
16	An opening or interval.	
17	A high-pitched bark.	
18	A device for catching an animal.	
19	An upper case letter.	
20	To hold captive perhaps for a ransom.	
21	What birds do with their wings.	
22	A round fruit with a core that grows on trees.	

Words with AP

Highlight the words with **AP** in the wordsearch.

Word bank

CHAP
CAPSIZED
SAP
CAPTAIN
CAP
CHAPTER
STRAP
COLLAPSE
WRAP
MAP
HAPPY
EVAPORATE
JAPAN
CAPSICUM
TAP
NAP
GAP
APPLE
TRAP
CAPITAL
KIDNAP
APPLY
FLAP
YAP

```
N M C C T K C A P S I Z E D W X
T E J A W K P B V Z Y C W V H G
Q V T W P A Y K W L C J K L W B
R A B Y L S R V Z G A P A F L Y
N P C F A B I C W N F T Z P L R
G O D Z C P N C H L M L P P A P
L R P H A Z A C U A K Y P B A N
G A X K P P P Z M M P A D N V Z
X T X P T J V G W A M T D T A C
W E M M A X C H S N P I E Y P B
F R P L I G H Q T K K W P R P J
M A A G N T A K R H A P P Y L T
C R Q P K K P P A K T R A P E W
W T A P Z W A Q P X L M K D Q M
N G M G C S C O L L A P S E G M
C A P I T A L N K T X G Z L H C
```

Write your highlighted **AP** words in alphabetical order in the table below.

1.	7.	13.	19.
2.	8.	14.	20.
3.	9.	15.	21.
4.	10.	16.	22.
5.	11.	17.	23.
6.	12.	18.	24.

Words with AT

AT has a short A phoneme and it is found most often in the first syllable of words, for example, *atom*, *category*, *gnat* and *gratitude*. When Y, ED, ER, EN and ING are added to one-syllable words with AT, the final T is doubled to keep the A phoneme short, for example, *bat – batted, batter, batting*; *flat – flatten* and *fat – fatty*.

Write the answers to these clues. Use the word bank to help you.

1. A man-made object orbiting a planet (9) _satellite_
2. A forked stick with a sling to fire missiles (8) _catapult_
3. Not 'this' (4) _that_
4. Level and smooth (4) _flat_
5. The grub of a moth or butterfly (11) _____
6. A planet with rings (6) _____
7. This is passed between runners in a relay (5) _____
8. An Australian burrowing marsupial (6) _____
9. A book of maps (5) _____
10. The day before Sunday (8) _____

Word bank

~~THAT~~
WOMBAT
BATON
ATLAS
SATURDAY
~~CATAPULT~~
CATERPILLAR
SATURN
~~SATELLITE~~
~~FLAT~~

Now fill in the word wall with your AT answers, using upper case letters.

1. S A T e l l i t e
2. C A T A P U L T
3. T H A T
4. F L A T
5. A T
6. A T
7. A T
8. A T
9. A T
10. A T

Words with AT

Sort these **AT** words according to their number of syllables.

diplomatic   gratitude   batter   mat   sat   atlas   satisfied
catapult   category   format   catamaran   catastrophic
acrobat   flatten   brat   atmosphere   material   fanatical
habitat   satin   rat   that   gnat   baton

 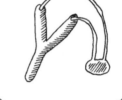 

1 syllable	2 syllables	3 syllables	4 syllables

The following two-syllable words have been muddled up. Join them together to create words with **AT**.

| at | matt | form | com |

| ress | bat | las | at |

Now do the same with these words which have more than two syllables.

| auto | demo | lat | flatt |

| itude | matic | ery | cratic |

Words with ET

ET has a short **E** phoneme and is commonly found at the end of words, for example, *bet, rocket, alphabet* and *forget.* When **Y, ED, ER** and **ING** are added to one-syllable words with **ET**, the final **T** is doubled to keep the **E** phoneme short, for example, *wet – wetter, wetted, wetting* and *pet – petty.*

Word bank

FIDGET	CRICKET
JACKET	BULLETS
ALPHABET	BLANKET
LOCKET	MET

Put the missing **ET** words in the sentences below.

1. My older brother loves to play _____ and he is a great bowler.

2. The soldiers stopped firing when they ran out of _____.

3. It was so cold I needed an extra _____ on my bed.

4. I have a silver _____ with a picture of my grandmother inside it.

5. I went to town and _____ my best friend to go shopping.

6. My dad wears a leather _____ when he rides his motorbike.

7. There are 26 letters in the _____.

8. My teacher hates it when we _____ and she tells us to sit still.

These two-syllable words all end in **ET**, but in the first syllable they have different, short vowel phonemes. Sort them, using the table below, according to the vowel phoneme in their first syllable.

 PACKET HELMET GADGET CRICKET ROCKET INLET GOBLET
TURRET CRUMPET LOCKET FILLET PELMET VELVET PELLET
PLANET MAGNET WICKET BONNET JUNKET BUDGET

A	E	I	O	U
BASKET	FERRET	MILLET	SOCKET	BUCKET

Words with ET

Complete this crossword using words that end with **ET**.

Word bank

JET	BRACELET
SET	FORGET
GULLET	TURRET
JUNKET	WET
PACKET	REGRET
WHIPPET	FILLET
SOCKET	MILLET
HELMET	HATCHET
CARPET	TRINKETS
CRUMPET	VET
RACKET	WALLET
NET	

ACROSS

1. A dog similar to a small greyhound (7)   **4.** A dessert made with milk and rennet (6)
7. A slice of meat or fish (6)   **8.** This is used to catch fish (3)   **9.** A man's purse (6)
12. A hard black rock or a type of aeroplane (3)   **13.** A small axe (7)   **14.** To become firm like jelly (3)   **19.** Heavy floor covering often made of wool (6)   **20.** A piece of jewellery worn on the arm (8)   **22.** An animal doctor (3)   **23.** A protective cover for the head (6)

DOWN

2. A small parcel or container (6)   **3.** A hole for something to fit in to (6)   **5.** Small ornaments (8)   **6.** A type of bird seed (6)   **10.** An antonym for remember (6)   **11.** To feel sorry or wish you hadn't done something (6)   **15.** A small tower (6)   **16.** An uproar or loud noise (6)   **17.** The food tube connecting the mouth to the stomach (6)
18. A soft cake eaten toasted with butter (7)   **21.** Not dry (3)

Words with IG

IG has a short **I** phoneme and it can be found in many words, for example, *dig, piglet* and *brigade*. When **Y, ED, ER** and **ING** are added to one-syllable words with **IG**, the final **G** is doubled to keep the **I** phoneme short, for example, *big – bigger; rig – rigged, rigging* and *pig – piggy*.

Solve the clues and then complete the crossword using upper case letters.

Word bank

PIG	PIGLET
RIG	SIGNAL
IGNORE	ZIGZAG
WIG	RIGGING
TWIG	VIGOROUS
DIG	SIGNATURE
CIGARETTES	IGNITE
IGUANA	WRIGGLE
FIGURE	TRIGGER
GIGGLE	SNIGGER
JIGSAW	IGNORANT

ACROSS
4. A picture puzzle with many small pieces (6)   **6.** A sign or gesture to convey information (6)   **7.** Squeeze this lever to fire a gun (7)   **8.** A small branch (4)   **13.** To laugh in a sly way (7)   **14.** To move with a twisting action (7)   **17.** To disregard (6)
18. To burn or set fire to something (6)   **19.** You do this with a spade (3)   **20.** People smoke these (10)   **22.** A person's name written by themselves (on a cheque) (9)

DOWN
1. A young pig (6)   **2.** To move along with sharp left and right turns (6)
3. Uneducated and lacking knowledge (8)   **5.** Artificial hair for the head (3)   **9.** A large tropical American lizard (6)   **10.** Strong, active and energetic (8)   **11.** A number or body shape (6)   **12.** Pork comes from this animal (3)   **15.** The ropes and sails of a ship (7)
16. To laugh, nervously perhaps (6)   **21.** The apparatus for drilling oil (3)

Words with IG

Sort these **IG** words according to their number of syllables in the table below.

PIG   RIG   IGNORE
WIG   TWIG   DIG   IGUANA
FIGURE   GIGGLE   JIGSAW
PIGLET   CIGARETTES   SIGNAL   ZIGZAG
RIGGING   VIGOROUS   SIGNATURE
IGNITE   WRIGGLE   TRIGGER
SNIGGER   IGNORANT

1 syllable	2 syllables	3 syllables

Words with IN

Write the answers to these clues in lower case letters.

1. The season before spring (6) _____
2. Interesting and delightful (11) _____
3. A container for rubbish (3) _____
4. Not fat (4) _____
5. Ideas, beliefs or feelings (8) _____
6. A broad smile (4) _____
7. A synonym for start (5) _____
8. An antonym for start (6) _____
9. Part of the face below the mouth (4) _____
10. New and not copied (8) _____

Sort your answers into different types of words in the table below. Some words belong in more than one group.

Noun – singular	Noun – plural	Verb	Adjective

Words with IN

Highlight the **IN** words in the wordsearch.

```
C G F T R L Y T N J M D W H
G H R A E Z N S I F H N S M
R R I S S I L R P N T I M I
I T N N O C F M M I N J I N
N I V C W B I Q I I N S N I
T W I N T E R N F N N C U B
O P I N I O N S A I I X T U
O R I G I N A L G T P M E S
B V Z T W N T R T K I H U G
E K K J I L A D H F R N X M
G K T B Y M T P I Q I L G N
I R A I S I N S N N L N I D
N Y R M D I N N E R P W S I
J X H P I N A F O R E K L N
```

Word bank

FINISH	MINIBUS
WINTER	WIN
FASCINATING	ORIGINAL
THIN	TIN
TINSEL	OPINIONS
RAISINS	BEGIN
SPIN	CHIN
DIN	MINUTE
MARGINS	FINS
DINNER	BIN
MINIMUM	GRIN
PINAFORE	

Write the answers to these clues in lower case letters.

1. Sixty seconds (6) _____
2. An antonym for lose (3) _____
3. Glittering metallic decoration (6) _____
4. A small bus (7) _____
5. Dried grapes (7) _____
6. To revolve quickly (4) _____
7. A metal used to make food containers (3) _____
8. Fish have these to help them swim (4) _____
9. The main meal of the day (6) _____
10. The borders on pages (7) _____
11. An antonym for maximum (7) _____
12. A dress with a bib top (8) _____
13. A continuous roar or racket (3) _____

Words with IP

IP has a short I phoneme and it can be found in many words, for example, *hips, skip* and *tulip*. IP is also part of the suffix SHIP which means 'a state of being', for example, *friend – friendship* and *owner – ownership*. When Y, ED, ER and ING are added to one-syllable words with IP, the final P is doubled to keep the I phoneme short, for example, *skip – skipper, skipped, skipping* and *hip – hippy*.

Write the answers next to the clues in lower case letters.
Then, complete the word wall using upper case letters.

1. A large boat. _____
2. The pointed end of something or a helpful piece of information. _____
3. A clothes fastener with two rows of teeth. _____
4. Fried potatoes or small pieces of something. _____
5. The written text of a play or film. _____
6. Makeup worn on the lips. _____
7. Soft, warm, indoor footwear. _____
8. Another name for fins used when swimming and snorkelling. _____
9. A hole, tear or a dangerous fast tide flowing out to sea. _____
10. A small hollow or a quick swim. _____

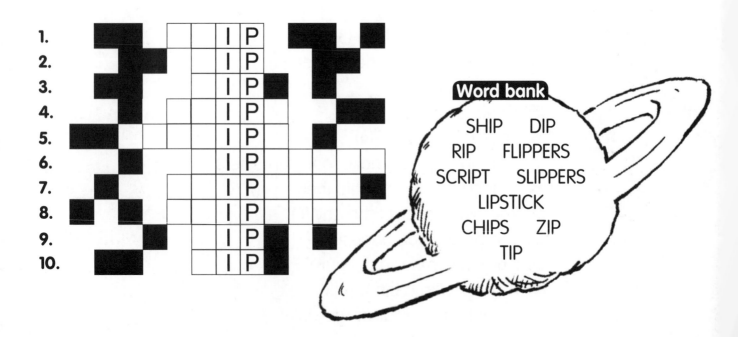

Word bank

SHIP   DIP
RIP   FLIPPERS
SCRIPT   SLIPPERS
LIPSTICK
CHIPS   ZIP
TIP

Words with IP

Write the correct **IP** words in these sentences.

Word bank

NIPPING	LIPS	SIP
WHIP	STRIP	CLIPS
HIPS	TRIP	FLIP
DRIPPING	RIPPLES	GRIP

1. My new trousers were the right size around the waist, but too big on the

   _____.

2. The puppy kept _____ people and it had to
   be trained not to bite.

3. To make a meringue you have to _____ the egg whites until they
   are stiff.

4. The nurse used a thin _____ of material, in place of a bandage.

5. When I was learning to ride my bike, I used to _____
   the handlebars really tightly with my hands.

6. My dog licks his _____ when he knows it's dinner time.

7. The leaky tap would not stop _____.

8. We went on a great _____ to Europe in the holidays.

9. The drinks were so hot, we had to _____ them
   slowly.

10. It was so calm, there were only little _____ on the water.

11. The _____ on the case were broken and it wouldn't close
    properly.

12. To turn a pancake over, if you are really clever, you can _____ it
    up into the air.

Words with IT

IT has a short I phoneme and it can be found in many words, for example, *kitchen*, *little* and *bit*. When **Y, ED, ER, EN** and **ING** are added to one-syllable words with **IT**, the final **T** is doubled to keep the I phoneme short, for example, *sit – sitter, sitting; bit – bitten* and *grit – gritty*. An exception to this is *pity* with only one **T**. Verbs with **IT** and only one syllable are often irregular in the past tense, for example, *sit – sat*, and *bit* is the past tense of *bite*.

Word bank

QUIT
SPIT
ARMPIT
BANDIT
KITTEN
SPIRIT
SUMMIT
CULPRIT
JITTERY
MITTENS
WITNESS
WRITTEN
IT
BIT
FIT
HIT
KIT
PIT
SIT
EXIT
GRIT
KNIT

ACROSS
3. Rough particles of sand (4)   **6.** A deep hole (3)   **8.** An outlaw or robber (6)
9. The hollow under the arm at the shoulder (6)   **11.** Recorded on paper in words, means '_ _ _ _ _ _ _ down' (7)   **13.** The informal word for saliva (4)   **14.** The top of a mountain (6)   **17.** Nervous and not calm (7)   **18.** To make use of a chair and not stand (3)   **20.** Healthy and well (3)   **21.** An antonym for entrance (4)

DOWN
1. To stop doing something (4)   **2.** Gloves without separate fingers (7)   **4.** If someone is 'full of _ _ _ _ _ _ _' they are lively and energetic (6)   **5.** To make clothes with wool and needles (4)   **7.** To strike with a blow or missile (3)   **10.** A short word for something with no name (2)   **11.** Someone who observes a crime (7)
12. Someone who is guilty of a crime (7)   **15.** A young cat (6)   **16.** The past tense of bite (3)   **19.** Equipment, an outfit or uniform (3)

Words with OP

OP has a short **O** phoneme and is found in many words, for example, *copper*, *poppy* and *flop*. When **Y**, **ED**, **ER** and **ING** are added to one-syllable words with **OP**, the final **P** is doubled to keep the **O** phoneme short, for example, *shop – shopper, shopped, shopping* and *flop – floppy*.

Find and circle the 16 **OP** words in this letter puzzle. The first one has been done for you.

heli copt er hop gall optop icmop pingcrop stop plehop op ticiantoph opp edchop pingco pydro pstopc rops

Unjumble the anagrams in brackets to find the answers to these clues.

1. Very small amounts of liquid. (SPORD) _____
2. Untidy and careless. (PLOPSY) _____
3. To cut with a sharp blow. (COPH) _____
4. The sound of horses' hooves 'clip _ _ _ _'. (PLOC) _____
5. A play in which all the words are sung. (PRAEO) _____
6. End or Finish. (POST) _____
7. To make negatives into photographs. (PLODEEV) _____
8. The sound made by a burst balloon. (PPO) _____
9. Liked by lots of people. (RALUPOP) _____

Using all the **OP** words from this page, sort them in the table below to show which syllable has the **OP** letter string. Three words have been written in to help you.

OP in 1st syllable	OP in 2nd syllable	OP in 3rd syllable
operation	wall**op**	helic**op**ter

Words with OT

OT has a short **O** phoneme and is found in words, such as, *robot, not* and *Scotland.* When **Y, ED, ER, EN** and **ING** are added to one-syllable words with **OT**, the final **T** is doubled to keep the **O** phoneme short, for example, *spotty, knotted, hotter, knotting* and *rotten.*

Write the answers next to the clues in lower case letters.

1. An orange edible root vegetable (6) _____
2. An orange coloured fruit not as big as a peach (7) _____
3. A small spot or mark (3) _____
4. The past tense of shoot (4) _____
5. A mechanical 'person' (5) _____
6. The study of plants (6) _____
7. The past tense of get (3) _____
8. Decomposed or decaying (6) _____
9. An election (6) _____
10. You can tie these with string (5) _____
11. Covered in dots or pimples (6) _____
12. You can brew tea in this (6) _____
13. A block of cast metal (gold perhaps) (5) _____

Highlight the words with **OT** in the wordsearch.

Word bank

BOTANY	THROTTLE
APRICOT	BOTTOM
BALLOT	JOT
SPOTTY	COTTON
INGOT	TROT
LOT	FORGOT
CARROT	TEAPOT
SHOT	KNOTS
GOT	ROTTEN
HOT	DOT
BOTTLE	ROBOT

```
C  J  B  Y  X  D  B  O  T  T  L  E  T
O  L  O  A  T  J  T  D  N  T  G  O  M
T  S  K  T  L  O  K  E  N  P  B  O  T
T  P  N  X  G  L  T  Q  M  O  T  O  M
O  O  O  L  G  T  O  L  R  T  G  K  N
N  T  T  P  O  F  N  T  O  N  F  J  G
J  T  S  R  H  O  T  B  I  X  N  Y  S
C  Y  T  H  R  O  T  T  L  E  N  Z  H
X  A  A  P  R  I  C  O  T  A  Z  J  O
T  T  R  D  K  G  V  M  T  X  D  R  T
Z  R  Z  R  O  Q  K  O  L  O  T  D  M
G  X  O  J  O  T  B  T  E  A  P  O  T
P  L  K  T  B  T  L  F  O  R  G  O  T
```

Words with UG

UG has a short U phoneme and it can be found in these words: *rugby*, *jug* and *dugout*. When **Y**, **ED**, **ER** and **ING** are added to one-syllable words with **UG**, the final **G** is doubled to keep the **U** phoneme short, for example, *muggy*, *mugger*, *mugged* and *mugging*.

Complete this crossword using **UG** words.

Word bank

DRUGS	DUGOUT
SLUG	JUGGLER
SMUG	LUGGAGE
MUGGY	DUG
PLUG	JUG
SNUG	LUG
NUGGET	MUG
THUG	PUG
RUGGED	RUG
UGLY	TUG
RUGBY	BUGS
SHRUG	GLUG

ACROSS

1. A performer who throws and catches lots of balls or objects (7)   **3.** A small snub-nosed dog (3)   **6.** Rough or uneven, for example, 'The mountain path was _ _ _ _ _ _ ' (6)   **8.** The sound of liquid being swallowed or poured out of a bottle (4)
10. An informal word for medicines (5)   **13.** A land snail without a shell that is a garden pest (4)   **15.** Bags and suitcases for travelling (7)   **16.** To pull hard or violently (3)   **17.** Small insects, germs or secret listening devices (4)   **19.** Damp, warm and humid weather (5)   **20.** A small floor mat (3)

DOWN

2. To pull or drag something along (3)   **3.** The stopper for the drainage hole in a sink (4)   **4.** This has a handle and spout and is used for pouring liquid (3)   **5.** A piece of gold (6)   **7.** The past tense of dig (3)   **9.** A violent person (4)   **10.** A boat made by hollowing out a log (6)   **11.** People do this with their shoulders to say 'I don't care or don't know' (5)   **12.** Similar to football, but with an oval ball (5)
13. Warm and cosy (4)   **14.** An antonym for pretty (4)   **18.** Self-satisfied or complacent (4)   **19.** A large cup with straight sides (3)

Words with UN

UN has a short **U** phoneme and it can be found in these words: *jungle, bun, mundane* and *uncle*. When **Y, ED, ER** and **ING** are added to one-syllable words with **UN**, the final **N** is doubled to keep the **U** phoneme short, for example, *funny, runner, stunned* and *stunning*. **UN** is also a prefix that can be added to words to make them mean the opposite, for example, *unhappy* and *unimportant*. Be careful with words beginning with **UNI** as this letter string changes **UN** into a long **U** phoneme.

Find and circle the 15 **UN** words in this letter puzzle. The first one has been done for you.

un der r unjun glehu ndr edpu nchstu nun easybun dle
und ersta ndun hap pybu nchfu nnyj unkd unge on
pu nct ure

Sort your answers into different types of words in the table below. One word belongs in more than one group.

nun underpants dunk punctual uncanny funny
chunks bun uncle gun skunks dungarees shun underline
munch bunkbeds puncture unhappy unfair

Noun – singular	Noun – plural	Verb	Adjective

Words with UN

Write the answers to these clues.

1. A childish name for a rabbit. _____
2. The athletes were _____ around the track.
3. A meal eaten at midday. _____
4. Crafty or sly; proverbs say a fox is _____.
5. This can be very loud and you hear it with lighting. _____
6. Two beds placed one on top of the other. _____
7. On time and not late. _____
8. Beneath the earth. _____
9. Not level or flat. _____
10. Not lucky. _____

Now, write your answers in the word wall.

29

Consonant blends with L

Consonant blends are created when two or more consonants are placed together. The words on this page have two letter blends with **L**. The blends can be at the beginning of the words (initial blends), for example, *pl*an, *fl*ame and *gl*are or in the middle, for example, camou*fl*age and neg*l*ect.

Blends in the middle are often found in compound words, for example, sun*gl*asses, cauli*fl*ower and over*fl*ow or after prefixes, for example, un*cl*ear, de*cl*are and re*pl*ace.

When a string of consonants are found in the middle of words, separating the words into syllables will make the words easier to read and spell. The following letters can go before **L** to make a consonant blend: **BL**, **CL**, **FL**, **GL**, **PL** and **SL**.

The words in this letter puzzle have blends with **L**. Find and circle the 12 words. The first one has been done for you.

sun flow er but terf lyre places tap lerp adlo ckp add ling

mul tip lyre pla yunc lears ungl as sest odd lero verf low

Unjumble the anagrams in brackets and write them on the lines.

1. Another word for an apartment is a _____. (LATF)
2. To quickly run away from something is to _____. (LEEF)
3. The sharp hooked nails of animals are _____. (WLACS)
4. The side of a hill or mountain is a _____. (POLES)
5. A _____ is a thick woollen bedcover. (BALTENK)
6. _____ help us to tell the time. (SCOCKL)
7. The coloured banners of countries are called _____. (GLAFS)
8. _____ help you find answers to crosswords and crimes. (SLUCE)
9. A plane that has no engine is a _____. (ERGLID)
10. A cut _____ until the blood clots. (DEEBLS)
11. A group of sheep is called a _____. (CKOFL)
12. People who wear _____ have problems with their eyes. (SEGSALS)

Consonant blends with L

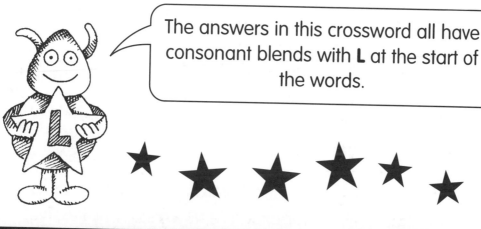

The answers in this crossword all have consonant blends with **L** at the start of the words.

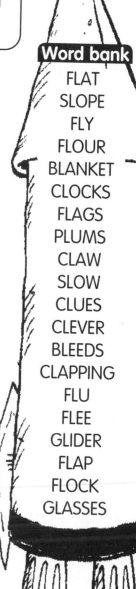

Word bank

FLAT
SLOPE
FLY
FLOUR
BLANKET
CLOCKS
FLAGS
PLUMS
CLAW
SLOW
CLUES
CLEVER
BLEEDS
CLAPPING
FLU
FLEE
GLIDER
FLAP
FLOCK
GLASSES

ACROSS

3. Another word for an apartment (4)   **5.** To quickly runaway from something (4)
6. The sharp hooked nail of an animal (4)   **7.** The side of a hill or mountain (5)
9. A thick woollen bedcover (7)   **12.** These help us tell the time (6)   **13.** The coloured banners of countries (5)   **16.** Round fruits with stones (5)   **17.** These help you find answers to crosswords and crimes (5)   **19.** A plane that has no engine (6)

DOWN

1. A cut does this, until the blood clots (6)   **2.** Not fast (4)   **4.** A synonym for applauding (8)   **5.** A group of sheep (5)   **8.** People with poor eyesight need these (7)
10. To move through the air like a bird or plane (3)   **11.** Brainy or intelligent (6)
14. Ground wheat powder used for making bread and cakes (5)   **15.** A bird's wings do this (4)   **18.** Short for influenza (3)

Consonant blends with R

Consonant blends are created when two or more consonants are placed together. The puzzle on this page has two-letter blends with **R**. The blends can be at the beginning of the words, for example, *train*, *brother* and *crowd* or in the middle, for example, *zebra*, *library* and *mongrel*.

Blends in the middle are often found in compound words, for example, *eardrum*, *footprint* and *foolproof* or after prefixes, for example, *undress*, *impressive*, *disgrace* and *increase*.

When a string of consonants are found in the middle of words, separating the words into syllables will make the words easier to read and spell. Here are some examples of blends with **R** to make these two-letter consonant blends: **BR, CR, DR, FR, GR, KR** (uncommon), **PR, WR** and **TR**. When **W** comes before **R** it is silent, for example, *write* and *wring*.

The answers to these clues are words with blends with **R**.

1. A flat board for carrying things (4) _____
2. Not wet (3) _____
3. Valuable things like gold or jewels (might be buried) (8) _____
4. A reward for winning (5) _____
5. Made from milk, can be whipped (5) _____
6. Used for sandwiches or toast (5) _____
7. A sleep fantasy (5) _____
8. To draw or copy exactly (5) _____
9. New, not stale (5) _____
10. An arch over a river (6) _____
11. The present tense of brought (5) _____
12. To attempt or test something out (3) _____
13. How much something costs (5) _____
14. To cook in oil (3) _____
15. A mate or buddy (6) _____
16. The wooden edges of pictures (6) _____
17. To turn to ice (6) _____
18. To shed tears (3) _____

Consonant blends with R

Highlight the words with the consonant blend **R** in the wordsearch.

Word bank

TRY   FRY   FRIEND
FRAMES   PRICE
FREEZE   CRY
TREE   PRIVATE   GREEDY
CREW   TRAY   DRY
TREASURE   PRIZE   CREAM
BREAD   DREAM   TRACE
FRESH   BRIDGE
BRING

T	R	E	A	S	U	R	E	Y	K	R	P
D	T	F	P	K	N	P	R	I	C	E	Q
R	F	R	R	R	W	G	R	E	E	D	Y
E	F	R	E	E	I	B	W	X	F	R	Y
A	R	C	E	E	E	Z	T	R	A	C	E
M	I	B	R	S	T	Z	E	B	M	E	D
T	E	R	C	E	H	T	E	S	T	E	T
C	N	I	R	P	W	V	E	A	G	D	R
R	D	N	Y	R	G	M	V	D	A	R	A
E	Z	G	R	Y	A	I	I	E	X	Y	Y
A	B	C	R	R	R	R	R	T	R	R	R
M	N	D	F	P	B	B	N	T	V	L	N

Unjumble the anagrams in brackets to find the words that have middle blends with **R** and write them on the lines.

1. Good looking or appealing. (VITECARTAT) _____
2. Wear this to keep clothes clean when cooking or painting. (RAPON) _____
3. A female actor. (SCATERS) _____
4. A frozen dessert eaten in a cone. (MICECARE) _____
5. This is used like a comb but it has bristles not teeth. (SHRUBIRAH) _____
6. Police collect and study these to identify criminals. No two are the same. (STINFINGRERP) _____
7. 10 x 10. (HUDERND) _____
8. A dog of mixed breeds, not a pedigree. (GLONERM) _____
9. To say yes or think the same as someone else. (ERAGE) _____
10. This is used to power lights and appliances. (TRICETILECY) _____

Consonant blends with W

Consonant blends are created when two or more consonants are placed together. The puzzle on this page has two-letter blends with **W**. These blends can be at the beginning of the words, for example, *swi*tch, *tw*enty and *dw*indle. They can also be found in the middle of compound words, for example, pig*sw*ill, or after prefixes, for example, up*sw*ing, be*tw*een and en*tw*ine. Only three letters can go before **W** to make a consonant blend: **SW**, **TW** and **DW**. Unusual words are *answer* and *sword* because the **W** is silent.

The words in this crossword all have blends with **W**.

Word bank

SWALLOW	SWIFT
TWINKLE	SWILL
TWITTER	TWICE
SWEEPING	TWIGS
SWINGING	TWINS
SWAMP	TWIRL
SWOTTING	TWIST
SWEATSHIRT	DWARF
SWEARS	SWANS
SWEETS	SWELLS
SWARM	TWELVE

ACROSS

4. A very large number of bees (5)   **7.** What stars do in the sky (7)   **9.** Grows larger (6)   **11.** A long sleeved, thick cotton jersey or jumper (10)   **12.** Moving to and fro on a child's playground activity (8)   **13.** Uses bad language (6)   **16.** Two children born together (5)   **17.** A small mythical person like an elf (5)   **18.** Another word for lollies, candies or desserts (6)   **19.** Two times (5)

DOWN

1. An area of wet marshy ground (5)   **2.** 10 + 2 (6)   **3.** Revising or studying for exams (8)   **5.** Small tree branches (5)   **6.** What birds do, making a noise (7)   **7.** To turn round quickly (5)   **8.** Using a broom to brush the floor (8)   **10.** Old food scraps that pigs eat (5)   **12.** What you do with food after you chew it (7)   **13.** A synonym for fast (5)   **14.** White water birds with long necks (5)   **15.** A type of dance with lots of turning (5)

Consonant blends with
C, K, M, N, P, Q and T

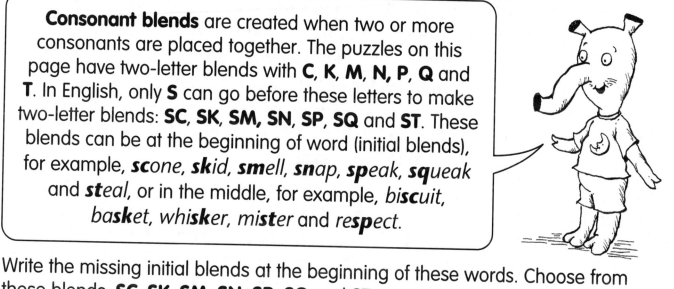

Consonant blends are created when two or more consonants are placed together. The puzzles on this page have two-letter blends with **C, K, M, N, P, Q** and **T**. In English, only **S** can go before these letters to make two-letter blends: **SC, SK, SM, SN, SP, SQ** and **ST**. These blends can be at the beginning of word (initial blends), for example, **sc**one, **sk**id, **sm**ell, **sn**ap, **sp**eak, **sq**ueak and **st**eal, or in the middle, for example, bi**sc**uit, ba**sk**et, whi**sk**er, mi**st**er and re**sp**ect.

Write the missing initial blends at the beginning of these words. Choose from these blends: **SC, SK, SM, SN, SP, SQ** and **ST**.

1. __ __ EEZE
2. __ __ OONS
3. __ __ IRRED
4. __ __ AIRS

5. __ __ ARTED
6. __ __ ARECROW
7. __ __ OWMAN
8. __ __ UARE

9. __ __ ORING
10. __ __ OTTY
11. __ __ UEEZE
12. __ __ IRT

13. __ __ ULL
14. __ __ ARLET
15. __ __ UIRREL
16. __ __ YSCRAPER

★ ★

Now write the missing blends in the middle of these words. Choose from these blends: **SC, SK, SM, SN, SP, SQ** and **ST**.

1. WHI __ __ ERS
2. DI __ __ USS
3. CU __ __ ARD
4. LOUD __ __ EAKER
5. TEA __ __ OON

6. SI __ __ ER
7. E __ __ APE
8. BA __ __ ET
9. E __ __ IMO
10. DI __ __ OVER

11. CON __ __ IRACY
12. IN __ __ ECT
13. OUT __ __ IRTS
14. RE __ __ UE
15. TRAN __ __ ORT

★ ★

Unjumble these anagrams to find words with **SC, SK, SM, SN, SP, SQ** and **ST**. The blends could be at the beginning or in the middle of words.

1. SCITFANTA _____
2. PEELSCOTE _____
3. MUTESOC _____
4. PARENTSRANT _____
5. SIDSIMS _____

6. SKEAN _____
7. MOTHSO _____
8. DRIPES _____
9. SHAQUS _____
10. MUGSLEG _____

Various consonant blends

Consonant blends are created when two or more consonants are placed together. The words in this puzzle have a variety of the two-letter blends. These blends can be at the beginning of the words, for example, **br**ing, **sn**ap and **sl**ip, or in the middle, for example, be**tw**een and re**pl**y.

Find the answers to the clues. Then, highlight words from the word bank in the wordsearch.

1. A caterpillar turns into this insect (9)   **2.** To answer by speaking or in a letter (5)
3. This device can pin pieces of paper together (7)   **4.** To speak very quietly (7)
5. These creatures have eight legs (7)   **6.** This spoon is bigger than a dessert spoon (10)   **7.** You see these in graveyards (7)   **8.** Tadpoles turn into these amphibians (5)   **9.** These twinkle in the sky at night (5)   **10.** Ladies can wear this to sleep in (10)   **11.** Dips and cavities on the moon (7)   **12.** To say that you are not pleased about something (8)   **13.** A building full of books that you can borrow (7)   **14.** Stick these on letters to pay for postage (6)   **15.** A woolly one keeps your neck warm (5)   **16.** You can tell the time with this (5)   **17.** An antonym for wet (3)   **18.** A very bad accident or misfortune (8)   **19.** To remove someone from a competition for breaking the rules (10)   **20.** Unable to see (5)

Q	S	C	M	N	H	Y	R	M	Y	B	X	M	S	R
Z	T	L	R	R	H	E	T	L	N	T	L	G	L	Y
S	A	O	X	C	P	S	F	O	N	P	O	A	F	L
T	R	C	K	S	R	R	O	L	T	R	W	R	D	G
A	S	K	I	E	E	P	Y	R	F	R	A	R	N	K
M	Z	H	D	T	S	L	S	V	E	C	U	T	D	D
P	W	I	T	E	Y	L	I	N	S	P	R	D	I	I
S	P	U	L	R	D	X	R	B	A	R	L	H	S	S
S	B	B	D	J	Z	Z	M	V	R	C	M	Y	A	Q
X	A	C	O	M	P	L	A	I	N	A	E	L	S	U
T	C	R	O	S	S	E	S	N	X	C	R	S	T	A
N	N	I	G	H	T	D	R	E	S	S	L	Y	E	L
X	B	L	I	N	D	D	K	W	H	K	Q	A	R	I
V	C	R	A	T	E	R	S	D	P	R	M	Y	B	F
X	T	R	Q	X	Z	S	T	A	P	L	E	R	M	Y

Word bank

BLIND	WHISPER
TABLESPOON	STAMPS
DISQUALIFY	BUTTERFLY
COMPLAIN	REPLY
STARS	CROSSES
SCARF	FROGS
DISASTER	LIBRARY
CLOCK	CRATERS
NIGHTDRESS	SPIDERS
STAPLER	DRY

Final consonant blends

Consonant blends are created when two or more consonants are placed together. The words in this puzzle contain a variety of consonant blends with the last letters **B, D, F, K, L, M, N, P** or **T**. These final blends can go after a short vowel phoneme, for example, *r**est***, or long vowel phoneme, ***ea**st*.

Read the clues to complete this crossword. Use the word bank to help you.

Word bank

BELT	FORK
HARD	CALM
RETURN	MASK
CURL	SUPERB
HELD	BEST
ALARM	THINK
BURN	HARP
HALF	SHARP
BULB	PALM
LAWN	PEARL
LEAST	DESCEND
STORM	TURN

ACROSS
2. This can give off light or plants can grow from it (4)   **7.** Very bad wet and windy weather is called a _ _ _ _ _ (5)   **8.** To come back (6)   **9.** You use your brain to do this (5)   **12.** The past tense of hold (4)   **13.** This is worn over the face for protection or as disguise (4)   **15.** To go down (7)   **17.** A very large stringed instrument (4)   **20.** A jewel that can be found in an oyster shell (5)   **21.** A type of tree that grows in tropical climates (4)   **22.** An antonym for worst (4)

DOWN
1. When the sea is _ _ _ _ there are no waves (4)   **2.** To scorch with a flame (4)   **3.** An antonym for most (5)   **4.** To change direction or rotate (4)   **5.** This goes with a knife (4)   **6.** People put rollers in their hair to make it do this (4)   **10.** An antonym for easy or soft (4)   **11.** An area of grass that needs to be mown (4)   **14.** Not blunt (5)   **16.** Wonderful or first class (6)   **17.** One of two equal parts (4)   **18.** This is worn around the waist (4)   **19.** In an emergency people raise the _ _ _ _ _ _ (5)

Words with a vowel before R

When **R** follows a vowel it changes the sound of the vowel, for example, *ban – barn*, *skit – skirt* and *am – arm*. All the vowels, **A, E, I, O** and **U**, can be followed by **R** to create the following: **AR, ER, IR, OR, UR**, for example, *cart*, *perfect*, *skirt*, *port* and *turn*. These can have different phonemes, for example, *pork – work* and *car – war*.

Write in the missing vowels in these words with vowel consonant digraphs.

1. M__RCH

2. N__RTH

3. P__RSON

4. TH__RD

5. CH__RCH

6. V__RNISH

7. M__RKET

8. W__RLD

9. CROSSW__RD

10. B__RD

11. K__RB

12. F__RRY

13. T__RCH

14. F__RNS

15. F__RMER

16. SQU__RM

Sort these words into rhyming groups in the table below. Be careful with words that start with **W**!

FOR STAR FORK HARM HEARD KERB HARD PALM BORN
TORN FIRM SHIRT FORT EXPORT TURN ARK YORK WORK
SQUIRM CHARM SMART TART WARN PSALM JERK SMIRK
FAR THIRD LEARN STIR YARD BLUR BLURB ALARM BLURT
ALERT HARP SNORT LARK WAR MORE HERB BIRD CORK
GERM BAR ART HER PARK BURN CARP LARD

OR	CAR	SHIRK	CALM	CORN	CART

CURB	WORD	PORK	FARM	WORM	HURT

CARD	FIR	DARK	FERN	SHARP	SHORT

Consonant digraphs

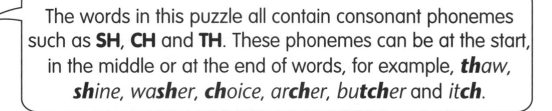

The words in this puzzle all contain consonant phonemes such as **SH**, **CH** and **TH**. These phonemes can be at the start, in the middle or at the end of words, for example, *thaw, shine, washer, choice, archer, butcher* and *itch*.

Word bank

BUSHES	CHEESE
SHELLS	WEATHER
WASH	BEACH
ASHES	FLASH
SHOES	CHURCH
SHIP	SHOP
PUSHING	KITCHEN
BUTCHER	THIRD
RASH	THEATRE
CHILD	RICH
MOTHER	SHUT
RUSH	WATCHES

ACROSS

1. A synonym for mum (6) **4.** A young person (5) **5.** Camera part, making a burst of light (5) **7.** One of three equal parts (5) **12.** Where plays are performed (7)
13. Spotty skin irritation (4) **14.** Closed, not open (4) **15.** A place to worship on Sundays (6) **20.** An antonym for pulling (7) **21.** A place where things are sold (4)
22. Large seagoing vessel (4) **23.** Made from milk, nice on toast (6) **24.** You can find these on the beach (6)

DOWN

2. A word meaning very wealthy (4) **3.** Someone who prepares and sells meat (7)
6. You wear them on your feet (5) **8.** A synonym for hurry (4) **9.** To clean with soap (4)
10. A room that people cook in (7) **11.** A synonym for observes or looks at (7)
16. This can be fine, sunny, wet or windy (7) **17.** The remains of anything burnt (5)
18. Plants, like small trees, often used for hedges (6) **19.** The sandy seashore (5)

Words with IGHT and ITE

Words with long **I** phonemes that end in **T** can only be spelt two ways: **ITE** or **IGHT**. **IGHT** is more common in one-syllable words. **ITE** is more common at the end of words with more than one syllable.

Write the answers to these clues. The first letter is provided for you and they all end in **IGHT** or **ITE**. Then, highlight these words in the wordsearch.

1. Not loose: T_____   **2.** Correct: R_____   **3.** Not dim: B_____   **4.** The present tense of fought: F_____

5. An antonym for heavy: L_____   **6.** A medieval soldier in armour: K_____   **7.** You need teeth to do this: B_____   **8.** To put pen to paper: W_____   **9.** An antonym for rude: P_____

10. The colour of snow: W_____   **11.** A toy that can be flown in the wind: K_____   **12.** To really please someone: D_____

13. A stony spike that hangs from the roof of a cave: S_____

14. A stony spike that grows up from the floor of a cave: S _____

L	B	X	S	A	T	E	L	P	I	N	E	F	Z	A
G	Z	I	T	R	I	G	H	T	F	R	W	Z	Y	P
D	S	F	T	L	W	L	K	X	F	N	J	V	N	D
E	T	I	P	E	T	R	M	X	V	K	Q	X	H	E
L	A	G	B	P	Y	F	I	F	G	H	W	H	T	T
I	L	H	B	N	R	T	R	T	W	H	I	T	E	I
G	A	T	P	R	H	P	E	T	E	K	Q	W	K	L
H	G	C	P	G	I	T	D	R	T	L	T	R	R	E
T	M	D	I	G	I	G	V	K	N	I	G	H	T	E
R	I	L	K	L	K	R	H	X	Y	R	Q	T	J	T
G	T	T	O	K	I	N	F	T	C	R	L	I	H	Y
B	E	P	G	K	T	W	H	B	Q	L	C	G	D	Q
Z	N	W	N	K	E	Z	M	R	K	E	I	L	K	C
V	M	N	X	T	M	P	F	H	R	T	B	T	B	W
G	Q	S	T	A	L	A	C	T	I	T	E	T	D	H

Word bank

RIGHT
BRIGHT
FIGHT
LIGHT
TIGHT
STALACTITE
KNIGHT
WRITE
BITE
DELIGHT
POLITE
WHITE
KITE
STALAGMITE

Homophones

A **homophone** is a word that is pronounced the same as another word, but with a different spelling and meaning, for example, *bored – board*, *weight – wait* and *toe – tow*.

For each homophone below there are two possible definitions. Put the answer next to the correct definition and write the missing homophone next to other definition.

1. **BEAR**: Naked _____ A furry animal _____
2. **BURY**: A fruit _____ To put underground _____
3. **HEAR**: To use your ears _____ Not there _____
4. **HI**: Not low _____ An informal greeting _____
5. **PIECE**: An antonym for war _____ A bit or part _____
6. **POOR**: An antonym for rich _____ To flow freely _____

For each example there is a choice of two homophones. Put the correct word next to the definition or into the sentence and write a sentence for the other word.

1. To slow down and stop. _____ (**brake, break**)

2. I _____ like to come, but I can't. (**wood, would**)

3. In the _____ people didn't have electricity. (**past, passed**)

4. During the _____ many soldiers were killed. (**war, wore**)

5. An amount, not exactly measured. _____ (**sum, some**)

6. This is often eaten for breakfast. _____ (**cereal, serial**)

7. I am going to _____ my shirt red. (**die, dye**)

8. I have already _____ that book. (**red, read**)

9. An elaborate chair for a king or queen. _____ (**throne, thrown**)

10. The _____ was in, so we could launch our boat. (**tied, tide**)

11. My naughty puppy _____ my slippers. (**chews, choose**)

Vowel digraphs

Digraphs are formed when two letters are placed together and pronounced with a single phoneme. Sometimes the digraph is created with two vowels, for example, **AU**, **OI** and **OU**. Sometimes the vowels are combined with consonants, for example, **AW**, **OW** and **OY**.

The vowel digraph heard in the words *pause* and *paws* can be spelt **AU** or **AW**.
● **AU** usually comes before **CE, D, ND, NT, T, NCH** and **G.**
● **AW** usually comes before **N** and **F**, or at the end of words.
● **AU** is never found before a vowel or at the end of words.

Read the clues and choose the correct digraph **AU** or **AW** for the answers. (The clues are not in order.) Write the words in the correct place in the word wall. Use the spelling hints above to help you.

★ Not cooked   ★ Children sit on this in a playground and go up and down
★ People do this when they are tired or bored   ★ A place where washing is done   ★ The season before winter   ★ A person who writes books
★ When the sun rises   ★ The month after July   ★ To praise by clapping
★ Visited by ghosts

Find and circle the eight **AU** and **AW** words in this letter puzzle. The first one has been done for you.

ca uses auc erpaw sdra waw fula uto matic cla wsl awn

42

Vowel digraphs

The vowel digraph heard in the words *cow* and *found,* can be spelt **OU** or **OW**.
● **OU** usually comes before **ND, NT, T, R, SE** and **TH**.
● **OW** usually comes before **N, EL, ER** and **L**, or at the end of words.
● **OU** is never found before a vowel or at the end of words.

Read the clues below and fill in the correct digraph **OU** or **OW** to complete the word.

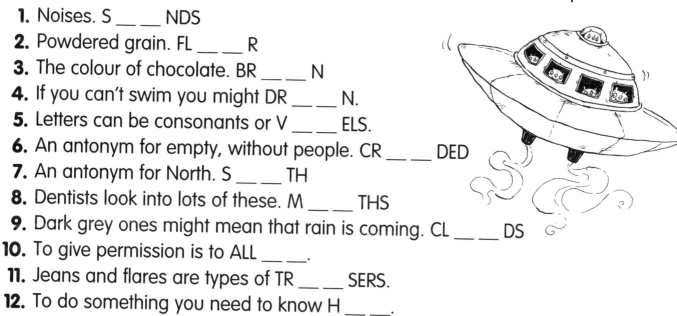

1. Noises. S __ __ NDS
2. Powdered grain. FL __ __ R
3. The colour of chocolate. BR __ __ N
4. If you can't swim you might DR __ __ N.
5. Letters can be consonants or V __ __ ELS.
6. An antonym for empty, without people. CR __ __ DED
7. An antonym for North. S __ __ TH
8. Dentists look into lots of these. M __ __ THS
9. Dark grey ones might mean that rain is coming. CL __ __ DS
10. To give permission is to ALL __ __.
11. Jeans and flares are types of TR __ __ SERS.
12. To do something you need to know H __ __.

The vowel digraph heard in the words *joy* and *join* can be spelt **OI** or **OY**.
● **OI** is usually found in the middle of words and **OY** is found at the end
● **OI** is never found before a vowel.

Choose the correct digraph **OI** or **OY** to complete the words below and write a
short clue or sentence for each one on a separate piece of paper.

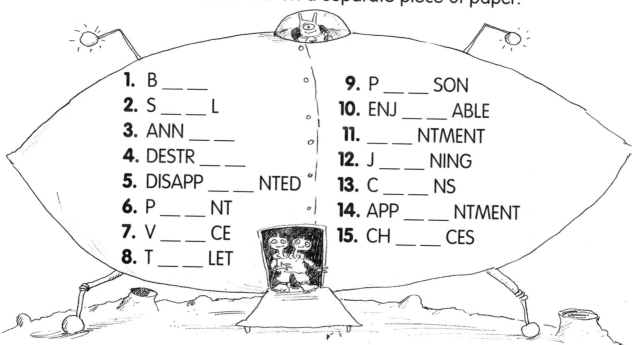

1. B __ __
2. S __ __ L
3. ANN __ __
4. DESTR __ __
5. DISAPP __ __ NTED
6. P __ __ NT
7. V __ __ CE
8. T __ __ LET

9. P __ __ SON
10. ENJ __ __ ABLE
11. __ __ NTMENT
12. J __ __ NING
13. C __ __ NS
14. APP __ __ NTMENT
15. CH __ __ CES

Long vowel phonemes

Long vowel phonemes are heard in these words: *make* and *week*. There are different ways of spelling these phonemes and the most common ones are shown below.

Long A phoneme
- **A_E** (with a silent **E** and different consonants), for example, *make, ape, ate, tale* and *game*.
- **AI** (vowel digraph followed by different consonants), for example, *tail, main, ailment* and *failure*.
- **AY** (vowel digraph often at the end of words), for example, *say, playground, Monday* and *display*.

Long E phoneme
- **EE** or **EA** (vowel digraph followed by different consonants or at the end of words), for example, *succeed, agree, meat* and *sea*.
- **E_E** (with a silent **E** and different consonants), for example, *scene, concrete* and *complete*.
- **E** (at the end of one-syllable words), for example, *be, me, she* and *he*.

Choose the correct spelling for these words with long **A** and long **E** phonemes and write a short sentence for each one on a separate piece of paper.

1. MAIK   MAKE   MAYK _____
2. GAIM   GAME   GAYM _____
3. AGAIN   AGANE   AGAYN _____
4. PLATIME   PLAITIME   PLAYTIME _____
5. SIXTEEN   SIXTEAN   SIXTENE _____
6. STREATS   STREETS   STRETES _____
7. GRENE   GREAN   GREEN _____
8. FREEDOM   FREADOM   FREDEOM _____

Long vowel phonemes

Long I phoneme
- **I_E** (with a silent **E** and different consonants), for example, *time, wide* and *drive*.
- **IGHT** (common letter string in one-syllable words), for example, *night* and *bright*.
- **IGH** (not as common as **GHT**), for example, *high, sigh* and *thigh*.
- **IE** (vowel digraph at the end of words), for example, *pie, tie* and *lie*.
- **Y**, for example, *sky, try, cycle, dye* and *type*.

Long O phoneme
- **O_E** (with a silent **E** and different consonants), for example, *hose* and *pole*.
- **OA** (vowel digraph followed by different consonants), for example, *goat* and *loaf*.
- **OW** (vowel digraph on its own or followed by different consonants), for example, *snow, bowl* and *grown*.
- **OE** (vowel digraph at end of words), for example, *toe, hoe* and *woe*.

Long U phoneme
- **U_E** (with a silent **E**), for example, *tube, duke, huge* and *cure*.
- **UE**, for example, *cue* and *due*.
- **EW**, for example, *few, dew, review* and *interview*.

Long vowel phonemes are heard in these words: *bike, hope* and *cube*. There are different ways of spelling these phonemes and the most common are below. Choose the correct spelling for these words with long **I**, long **O** and long **U** phonemes and write a short sentence for each one on a separate piece of paper.

1. WHITE   WIGHT _____
2. NITE   NIGHT _____
3. FLY   FLIGH   FLIE _____
4. SMILE   SMYLE   SMIEL _____
5. TIPTOES   TIPTOWS   TIPTOAS _____
6. CLOSED   CLOASED   CLOWSED _____
7. FOLLOW   FOLLOE _____
8. BARBECUE   BARBECEW _____
9. FULE   FUEL   FEWL _____
10. NEPTUNE   NEPTEWN   NEPTUEN _____

Words with a double consonant and LE

The words in these puzzles all have a double consonant followed by **LE**. They can be nouns, for example, *apple* and *riddle*, or verbs, for example, *wiggle* and *paddle*. The double consonant keeps the vowel short, for example compare the words, *gable* and *gabble*. When nouns, with a double consonant and **LE**, become plurals they just take an **S**, for example, *apple – apples*.

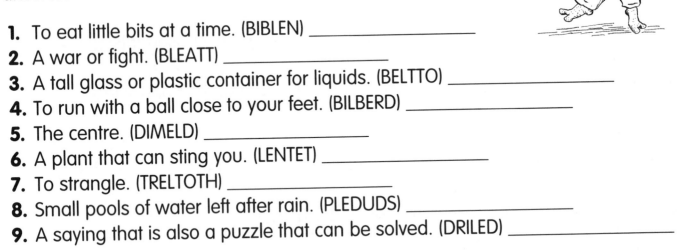

Unjumble these anagrams in brackets to find the words that have a double consonant followed by **LE** and write your answers on the lines.

1. To eat little bits at a time. (BIBLEN) _____
2. A war or fight. (BLEATT) _____
3. A tall glass or plastic container for liquids. (BELTTO) _____
4. To run with a ball close to your feet. (BILBERD) _____
5. The centre. (DIMELD) _____
6. A plant that can sting you. (LENTET) _____
7. To strangle. (TRELTOTH) _____
8. Small pools of water left after rain. (PLEDUDS) _____
9. A saying that is also a puzzle that can be solved. (DRILED) _____

 FIDDLE   CUDDLE   HOBBLE   STUBBLE
WRIGGLE   MUDDLE   RIPPLES   SKITTLES   PUZZLE

Write the missing words that have a double consonant followed by **LE** in these sentences. Use the words above to help you.

1. At the bowling alley we tried to knock down all the _____. (8)
2. Worms like to _____ through the soil. (7)
3. I was in such a _____ I didn't know where to begin. (6)
4. Another name for a violin is a _____. (6)
5. The elderly man with the bad leg began to _____ down the road. (6)
6. My mum gives me a _____ when I am feeling sad. (6)
7. Men shave their faces to get rid of their _____. (7)
8. The waves were so small they were only _____. (7)
9. A crossword is a type of word _____. (6)

Words with two syllables and two consonants in the middle

Words that have two syllables and two consonants in the middle usually have a short vowel phoneme in the first syllable. These pairs of words illustrate this rule: *biting – b**i**tten* and *filing – f**i**lming.*

Complete these sentences and then highlight the answers in the wordsearch.

1. My brother had chicken pox and was very _____. (6)   **2.** My big sister is really _____ and she is always telling me what to do. (5)   **3.** At the fair we love to eat _____ apples. (6)   **4.** In the mornings, my mum loves a cup of _____. (6)   **5.** The gardener has to _____ the seeds evenly on the ground. (7)   **6.** My favourite movies are _____ with cowboys in them. (8)   **7.** The farmer wanted to _____ the turkeys ready for Christmas. (6)   **8.** I love chips with fish in crispy golden _____. (6)   **9.** I was scared and excited when I went on the helter _____ at the fair. (7)   **10.** When people meet they usually say hi, _____ or a similar greeting. (5)   **11.** When bananas turn from green to _____ then they are ripe. (6)   **12.** The icing was too _____ and it slipped off the cake. (5)

T	F	J	H	F	V	I	T	T	E	R	T	E
S	K	E	L	T	E	R	P	H	E	L	E	R
W	E	S	T	E	R	N	S	E	R	F	E	P
F	A	T	T	E	N	K	F	E	F	T	L	X
B	A	T	T	E	R	F	T	O	T	H	B	Y
V	B	M	Z	L	O	K	C	A	F	M	U	V
N	O	F	L	T	E	R	C	C	F	C	T	X
K	S	K	L	B	S	S	Y	F	L	R	J	K
G	S	T	Q	K	P	H	C	E	U	W	E	N
B	Y	X	W	L	O	L	E	R	L	D	R	C
R	U	N	N	Y	T	M	L	L	C	L	N	D
Y	K	H	N	N	T	K	X	T	L	G	O	Y
Q	H	C	M	T	Y	L	H	R	R	O	B	W

Word bank

TOFFEE	SKELTER
BATTER	RUNNY
HELLO	BOSSY
SPOTTY	COFFEE
SCATTER	FATTEN
YELLOW	WESTERNS

Regular plurals and nouns that end in Y

When we make a **noun** into a plural we add **S**, for example, *bed – beds* and *house – houses*. When the noun ends in **Y** we have to be more careful and follow the rules:

● Final consonant followed by **Y** – remove the **Y** and add **IES**, for example, *puppy – puppies* and *party – parties*.
● Final vowel **Y** – keep the **Y** and add **S**, for example, *toy – toys* and *convoy – convoys*.

Write the missing nouns in this table and highlight them in the wordsearch. Some of them are plurals of words that end in **Y**.

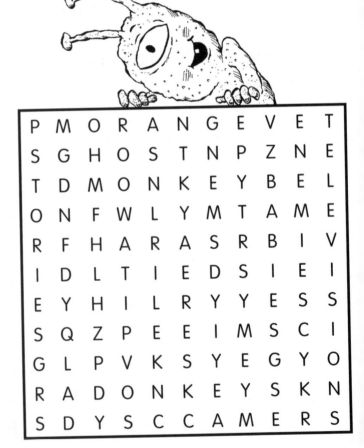

Singular noun	Plural noun
key	
	ghosts
	ladies
baby	
apple	
	donkeys
fairy	
story	
	tries
	oranges
enemy	
fly	
	monkeys
	televisions

P	M	O	R	A	N	G	E	V	E	T
S	G	H	O	S	T	N	P	Z	N	E
T	D	M	O	N	K	E	Y	B	E	L
O	N	F	W	L	Y	M	T	A	M	E
R	F	H	A	R	A	S	R	B	I	V
I	D	L	T	I	E	D	S	I	E	I
E	Y	H	I	L	R	Y	Y	E	S	S
S	Q	Z	P	E	E	I	M	S	C	I
G	L	P	V	K	S	Y	E	G	Y	O
R	A	D	O	N	K	E	Y	S	K	N
S	D	Y	S	C	C	A	M	E	R	S

48

Regular plurals and nouns that end in Y

Read the clues. Write in the plurals and nouns that end in **Y**. Then highlight your answers in the wordsearch. Use the word bank to help you.

1. These are on the roofs of houses and smoke comes out of them (8)

_____

2. Children play with these (4) _____

3. These people sneak around watching others (5) _____

4. An antonym for girls (4) _____

5. The cats and dogs home looked after lots of (6) _____

6. These are sometimes called sweets or candy (7) _____

7. There are seven of these in a week (4) _____

8. In rugby, it is good to score lots of these (5) _____

9. These are a form of transport that can carry lots of people across water (7)

_____

10. We wear clothes to cover our (6) _____

11. In the art gallery and museum there were lots of _____ to look at (8)

12. Waiters use these to carry food and drinks (5) _____

M	N	D	I	S	P	L	A	Y	S
C	H	I	M	N	E	Y	S	A	T
L	T	M	E	H	A	C	P	D	O
O	E	D	A	Y	S	E	I	B	Y
L	F	E	Y	D	S	H	E	O	S
L	G	L	O	E	K	J	S	D	O
I	M	T	I	B	O	Y	S	I	T
E	I	R	L	N	U	W	A	E	R
S	T	R	A	Y	S	Z	V	S	A
S	F	E	R	R	I	E	S	I	Y
A	I	S	L	B	I	M	A	T	S

Word bank

STRAYS
CHIMNEYS
TOYS
TRAYS
TRIES
BODIES
DISPLAYS
DAYS
LOLLIES
FERRIES
BOYS
SPIES

Verbs that end in Y

Look what happens to the verbs *worry* and *enjoy*, when the person who is doing the action changes:

- *I worry about exams. She/he worries about exams. We worry about exams. They worry about exams.*
- *I enjoy sport. She/he enjoys sport. We enjoy sport. They enjoy sport.*

When the verb ends in **Y** we have to follow these rules:

- Consonant before **Y** – remove the **Y** and add **IES**, for example, *worry* – *worries*.
- Vowel before **Y** – keep the **Y** and add **S**, for example, *enjoy* – *enjoys*.

Write in the missing verbs in this table and then put them into a sentence.

Verb	Verb with S	Sentence
carry		
	plays	
delay		
	fries	
envy		
	dries	
destroy		
multiply		
	disobeys	
hurry		

Change the verbs in the clues to the form that ends in **S**. Write your answers in the crossword. Then write a short sentence for each answer on a separate sheet of paper.

ACROSS
1. repay
6. reply
8. empty

DOWN
2. employ
3. delay
4. deny
5. stay
7. cry

Take off the E when you add ING

If a word ends with an **E**, when you add **ING** you must remove the **E** first, for example, *dance – dancing, charge – charging, drive – driving* and *file – filing*.

Read the clues and add **ING** to the words in the word bank to complete the crossword.

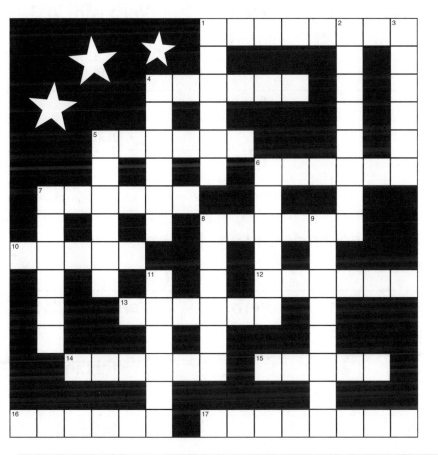

Word bank	
DIVE	NOTE
FACE	NOTICE
FADE	RIDE
FAKE	ROTATE
FIRE	SAVE
GIVE	TAKE
ICE	TIRE
INVITE	CHANGE
LIKE	USE
LIVE	WAVE
MAKE	WIPE
MOVE	

ACROSS
1. Turning round or spinning (8)
4. It means the colour is getting lighter (6)
5. Running out of energy (6)
6. Cleaning with a cloth (6)
7. Pretending and not being genuine (6)
8. Not being still (6)
10. Made of sugar and put on a cake (5)
12. Writing information in a quick way (6)
13. A synonym for enjoying (6)
14. You can do this off a high board (6)
15. Operating (5)
16. The opposite of spending or wasting (6)
17. Not staying the same (8)

DOWN
1. You do this on a horse (6)
2. Asking people to come to an event (8)
3. The opposite of taking (6)
4. It could mean sacking or shooting (6)
5. An antonym for giving (6)
6. Moving your hand to say goodbye (6)
7. Looking at something head on (6)
8. Another word for creating (6)
9. Observing or seeing something (8)
11. An antonym for dying (6)

Verbs with ING

The following words have short vowel phonemes and have two consonants or more at the end, so just add **ING**.

Verb	Verb with ING		Verb	Verb with ING
walk			jump	
	whisking			earning
punch			twirl	
	owning			painting
lick			hiss	
	messing		vanish	

The following words have short vowel phonemes and one final consonant.
Double the final consonant and add **ING**.

Verb	Verb with ING		Verb	Verb with ING
whip			mop	
	drumming			stabbing
scrub			bob	
	bugging			skidding
rip			flap	
	clipping			knotting

The following verbs have **Y** on the end so you can just add **ING**.

Verb	Verb with ING		Verb	Verb with ING
stay			employ	
	flying		defy	
disobey				obeying
	destroying		marry	
worry			deny	
pry				buying

Verbs with ING

Adding **ING** to the end of a verb makes the action described continuous, for example, *I am* **working** *today. I was* **working** *yesterday. I will be* **working** *tomorrow.*

Add **ING** to the clues and then write them in the crossword.

ACROSS	DOWN
2. wave _____	**1.** marry _____
7. slip _____	**2.** watch _____
8. add _____	**3.** delay _____
10. betray _____	**4.** reply _____
11. stray _____	**5.** agree _____
12. chop _____	**6.** worry _____
15. explode _____	**9.** display _____
16. fry _____	**13.** skip _____
17. pass _____	**14.** lock _____
18. shrug _____	
19. munch _____	

Irregular past tense verbs

Most past tense verbs end in **ED**, for example, *Yesterday I hopp**ed** and skipp**ed***. These are regular verbs. Unfortunately, some verbs are not regular and they do not end in **ED**. These irregular verbs need to be learned, for example, *I **run** away – I **ran** away* and *I **catch** the ball – I **caught** the ball*.

Write the past tense for the following irregular verbs. Then highlight them in the wordsearch.

Present tense	Past tense		Present tense	Past tense
have			understand	
am			wear	
go			run	
eat			steal	
do			buy	
see			bring	
think			hit	
write			grow	
sit			shake	
stand			freeze	
shine			bite	
take			throw	

T	K	M	K	V	W	O	R	E	C	M	H
H	H	W	R	O	T	E	G	R	E	W	I
O	U	F	S	D	S	T	O	L	E	F	T
U	N	N	I	H	B	R	O	U	G	H	T
G	S	D	D	S	O	K	S	H	O	N	E
H	T	N	A	E	O	O	K	R	N	T	J
T	O	W	K	O	R	V	K	A	A	T	E
T	O	G	T	F	L	S	R	S	H	T	W
H	D	P	G	L	R	Z	T	G	A	Q	E
R	H	A	D	B	T	O	U	O	S	N	N
E	M	L	L	I	D	O	Z	F	O	A	T
W	P	M	D	T	B	P	B	E	M	D	W

Nouns (male and female)

Nouns are naming words and some of them have male and female forms, for example, *lord – lady* and *man – woman*. The suffix **ESS** can also be added to nouns to make the female form, for example, *mayor – mayo**ress***. Sometimes the male form of the noun changes a little before **ESS** is added, for example, *wait**er** – wait**ress***. There are some words that sound like they might be female nouns but they are not, for example, *impress*, *express* and *undress*.

Find the matching pairs of nouns in this list and write them in the table below.

 lion   princess   actor   headmaster   duchess   woman
lioness   duke   actress   prince   man   headmistress

	Male	Female		Male	Female
1.			4.		
2.			5.		
3.			6.		

Each noun in the word bank is missing its partner. Highlight the missing words in the wordsearch. Then, on a separate piece of paper, sort them into two groups: 'Male' and 'Female'.

```
S M T F D H O S T E S S
I B E A L L T U N F N P
S R M T N K O R N A O N
T F P H J F G R M C U X
E X E E P C C O D N L T
R B R R T L W W B M G E
N N O C R R W A I T E R
E G R I I N L K N K Q T
I T G A E D Q Q Y W T L
C N H E C O U N T V L L
E C U T I G R E S S V Z
Z Q M A N A G E R E S S
```

Word bank

1. KING
2. COUNTESS
3. LADY
4. NEPHEW
5. CHAIRMAN
6. WAITRESS
7. HOST
8. AUNT
9. EMPRESS
10. TIGER
11. MONK
12. VIXEN
13. MOTHER
14. BROTHER
15. BOY
16. MANAGER

Suffixes that can be added to verbs and nouns to make adjectives

Adjectives are words that describe nouns. The suffixes **ABLE, IC, FUL, LESS, ING, LIKE, IVE** and **WORTHY** can be added to verbs and nouns to make adjectives, for example, *regret – regret**able**, hero – hero**ic**, use – use**ful**, glow – glow**ing*** and *blame – blame**worthy***. Sometimes the verbs have to be changed a little before the suffix is added, for example, *off**end** – offens**ive**, fantas**y** – fantast**ic*** and *regret – regret**able***.

Add a suffix to the verbs and nouns in the clues to make them into adjectives. Then complete the crossword. Remember, some verbs need to be changed first!

ACROSS

1. THANK_____
6. CHILD_____
7. DETACH_____

8. SNARL_____
9. HOPE_____
11. DISTRUST_____

16. PERSUADE_____
17. THOUGHT_____
18. AVOID_____

19. GUSH_____
20. CRY_____

DOWN

2. FORGET_____
3. WONDER_____
4. PRAISE_____

5. CARE_____
10. GLOW_____
11. DOUBT_____

12. DECIDE_____
13. WARN_____
14. METAL_____

15. ALLOW_____
16. PLAY_____

Suffixes that can be added to nouns to make verbs

The suffixes **ATE**, **IFY** and **ISE** can be added to nouns to change them into verbs, for example, *pulse – puls**ate**, class – class**ify** and terror – terror**ise**.* Sometimes the nouns have to be changed before the suffix is added, for example, *beauty – beaut**ify** and critic**ism** – critic**ise**.*

Add the suffixes **ATE**, **IFY** or **ISE** to the nouns in the clues to make them into verbs. Then write your answers in the crossword.

ACROSS
1. ADVICE   **6.** RELATION   **7.** SPECIALITY   **11.** TERROR   **12.** COMMUNICATION
16. VANDAL   **17.** DEVICE   **18.** INVESTIGATION   **19.** IMPLICATION

DOWN
2. IDOL   **3.** HORROR   **4.** NOTE   **5.** REALITY   **8.** PUNCTUALITY   **9.** CLASS
10. VACATION   **13.** MIGRANT   **14.** ADVERT   **15.** IDENTITY

The suffixes AL, ARY, IC, SHIP, HOOD, NESS and MENT

All these suffixes have similar meanings, which are 'having the nature of', 'related to' or 'state of being'. Words with these suffixes can be nouns or adjectives:

- Nouns: *rehearsal*, *commentary*, *friendship*, *motherhood*, *bitterness* and *settlement*.
- Adjectives: *angelic*, *customary* and *medical*.

Add the correct suffix (**AL, ARY, IC, SHIP, HOOD, NESS** or **MENT**) to these root words.

1. rude_____
2. diction_____
3. sign_____
4. leader_____
5. athlet_____

6. champion_____
7. move_____
8. hero_____
9. amaze_____
10. child_____

11. moment_____
12. music_____
13. brother_____
14. weak_____

Highlight the words in the word bank in the wordsearch.

Word bank

IDLENESS
REFRESHMENT
POETIC
FRIENDSHIP
OPTICAL
FALSEHOOD
GEOMETRIC
LIBRARY
KNIGHTHOOD
MEDICAL
CUSTOMARY
SPORTMANSHIP
SWEETNESS
MEASUREMENT

R	E	F	R	E	S	H	M	E	N	T	M	H	L	L
K	M	J	K	T	M	T	I	D	L	E	N	E	S	S
B	E	F	K	H	Y	T	R	L	N	Q	N	L	K	S
H	A	F	R	I	E	N	D	S	H	I	P	G	Z	P
N	S	N	B	L	P	G	Y	R	R	Q	R	K	Z	O
G	U	P	F	A	L	S	E	H	O	O	D	K	X	R
E	R	C	N	P	L	K	Q	K	S	D	Y	N	C	T
O	E	X	O	R	O	P	J	S	Z	R	Y	I	B	S
M	M	L	B	P	M	E	E	R	A	B	L	G	C	M
E	E	P	I	L	T	N	T	M	T	A	K	H	G	A
T	N	R	X	B	T	I	O	I	C	L	R	T	G	N
R	T	M	F	E	R	T	C	I	C	N	D	H	J	S
I	R	M	E	L	S	A	D	A	H	X	B	O	L	H
C	X	W	M	U	K	E	R	X	L	Q	K	O	C	I
W	S	G	C	M	M	T	L	Y	K	V	W	D	L	P

The suffixes IBLE and ABLE

The suffixes **IBLE** and **ABLE** mean 'capable of' or 'able to be'. They are added to make words into adjectives, for example, *accept – acceptable*. The rule for adding these suffixes is as follows:

- **ABLE** is usually added to complete words, for example, *value – valuable*.
- **IBLE** is usually added to roots that are not complete words, for example, *horr – horrible*.

Add the suffix **ABLE** or **IBLE** to the words in the word bank and then highlight them in the wordsearch.

```
M  P  P  O  S  S  I  B  L  E  D  J  M  P  D  T  Z  R  G
L  P  C  F  V  I  N  V  I  S  I  B  L  E  K  I  L  J  K
N  A  N  O  L  R  E  G  R  E  T  T  A  B  L  E  B  K  B
V  H  U  G  M  E  L  B  E  L  I  E  V  A  B  L  E  L  B
I  T  F  G  N  P  X  L  J  K  C  J  J  Z  J  Q  L  K  E
N  H  X  Z  H  K  A  I  P  K  M  Q  J  L  X  T  Y  G  T
C  V  K  R  P  A  J  R  B  R  B  R  E  A  K  A  B  L  E
R  A  R  E  U  J  B  C  A  L  E  G  M  E  L  M  W  N  T
E  R  E  S  N  L  Z  L  V  B  E  F  L  L  C  P  L  G  T
D  S  L  P  I  M  B  M  E  L  L  B  E  E  H  D  F  E  E
I  P  I  O  S  W  X  Y  W  K  A  E  L  R  E  D  L  T  R
B  O  A  N  H  V  V  J  N  N  K  B  E  L  A  B  C  N  R
L  N  B  S  A  P  G  C  O  F  I  L  B  D  A  B  F  N  I
E  X  L  I  B  M  Z  S  N  R  B  A  P  R  T  K  L  K  B
M  I  E  B  L  V  A  V  R  A  D  L  A  Y  M  T  M  E  L
N  B  T  L  E  E  L  O  R  I  K  E  B  Q  B  M  Y  K  E
R  L  K  E  R  N  H  O  O  V  B  M  G  R  P  L  P  B  R
Z  E  J  L  R  H  D  V  H  N  E  D  I  B  L  E  K  J  P
W  W  N  N  T  A  A  R  L  T  M  C  V  M  P  Z  P  J  M
```

Word bank

ADORE
BREAK
COMPARE
PUNISH
REASON
REGRET
PREFER
BEAR
BELIEVE
LAUGH
RELY
AVOID
POSS
FLEX
TERR
HORR
INVIS
RESPONS
ED
INCRED

The suffix ION

The suffix **ION** changes verbs into nouns and means the 'act', 'state', 'result' or 'process of'. The words on this page all end in **TION** or **SION**. **TION** is pronounced **SHUN**, for example, *action*. **SION** is pronounced a bit like **ZHUN**, for example, *decision*. **TION** is added to words with the letter string **UTE**, for example, *pollute – pollution*. **SION** is added to words with the letter string **USE** or **UDE**, for example, *confuse – confusion*.

Add the correct suffix **TION** or **SION** to the clues and complete the crossword.

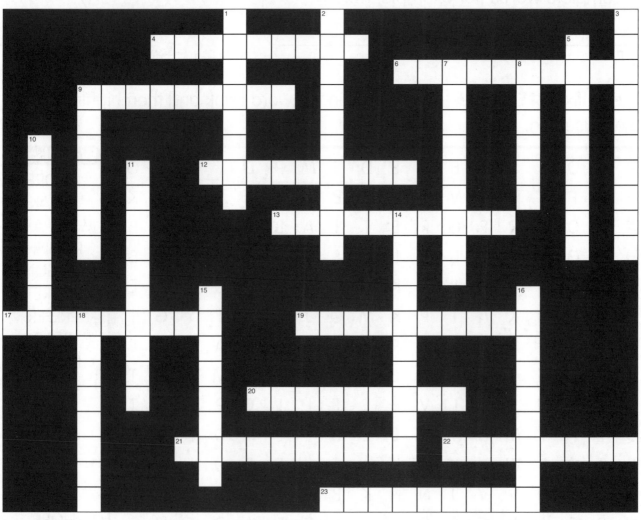

ACROSS
4. DIRECT (9)   **6.** DECORATE (10)   **9.** EDUCATE (9)   **12.** CONFUSE (9)   **13.** PROTECT 10)
17. INFECT (9)   **19.** SUSPEND (10)   **20.** EXPLODE (9)   **21.** CORRECT (10)   **22.** DIVIDE (8)
23. AFFECT (9)

DOWN
1. DECIDE (8)   **2.** CONCLUDE (10)   **3.** CONNECT (10)   **5.** DIGEST (9)   **7.** COLLIDE
(9)   **8.** ACT (6)   **9.** ERODE (7)   **10.** REVISE (8)   **11.** PREVENT (10)   **14.** COLLECT (10)
15. INVADE (8)   **16.** INVENT (9)   **18.** ELECT (8)

The prefixes A, AL, BE, IN and TO

Prefixes are added to the start of words. These prefixes have the following meanings:
- **A** means 'on', for example, *aboard* = *onboard*;
- **AL** is a shortened form of 'all', for example, *already* = *all ready*;
- **BE** means 'be', 'to' or 'by the', for example, *beside* = *to the side*;
- **IN** means 'in', for example, *inside* (Be careful though as **IN** can sometimes make a word mean the opposite: *accurate* – *inaccurate*.);
- **TO** means 'this', for example, *today* = *this day*.

Add the correct prefixes (**A, AL, BE, IN** or **TO**) and write the complete words in the gaps so that the sentences make sense.

1.	_____most	Wait for me; I won't be long as I am _____ ready.
2.	_____night	I am going out _____, so I must get home from work early.
3.	____together	There are one hundred pupils in my school _____.
4.	_____ware	The sign on the garden gate said '_____ of the dog'.
5.	_____doors	It started to rain, so we went _____ until it stopped.
6.	_____land	As we drove _____ we could no longer hear the waves.
7.	_____ready	We were late and when we got there the game had _____ started.
8.	_____day	I didn't sleep well last night so I am really tired _____.
9.	_____fore	It is important to clean your teeth _____ you go to bed.
10.	_____shore	We jumped out of the little boat and waded _____.
11.	_____low	We had to write our names at the bottom of the paper _____ our pictures.
12.	_____part	We were not allowed to sit together, we had to sit _____.

The suffixes OUS and IOUS

The suffixes **OUS** and **IOUS** are pronounced '**US**' and '**IUS**'. Usually you can hear the difference between the two, for example, *porous* and *glorious*. **S**oft **C**, **T** and **X** are usually followed by **IOUS**, for example, *vicious, infectious* and *anxious*. When the suffixes **OUS** and **IOUS** are added, the root word is sometimes clear, for example, <u>*adventure*</u> – <u>*adventurous*</u>, <u>*infect*</u> – <u>*infectious*</u> but this is not always the case.

Circle the seven **OUS** and **IOUS** words in this letter puzzle. The first one has been done for you.

obno   xiou   stedio   usmis   chi   evo   usmar   vellous

glo   rio   uslux   uriou   smys   teri   ous

Add the correct suffix **IOUS** or **OUS** to the following words and write the complete word on the lines. Say each ending out loud and see which sounds right or check in a dictionary.

1. suspic _____

2. vigor _____

3. nerv _____

4. tremend _____

5. hilar _____

6. obv _____

7. ridicul _____

8. fam _____

9. fur _____

10. prec _____

Add the missing vowels to the following words ending in **OUS** and **IOUS**. The vowels you need are in the brackets.

1. n__t__r__ __ __s (**i o o o u**)

2. __dv__nt__r__ __s (**a e o u u**)

3. s__p__rst__t__ __ __s (**e i i o u u**)

4. v__n__m__ __s (**e o o u**)

5. __nf__ct__ __ __s (**e i i o u**)

6. r__l__g__ __ __s (**e i i o u**)

7. r__v__n__ __s (**a e o u**)

8. __nc__nsc__ __ __s (**i o o u u**)

62

The suffixes OUS and IOUS

Read the clues and add the correct beginning to these **OUS** and **IOUS** words. Write the words on the lines.

1. Huge (8) _____ OUS
2. Important and not funny (7) _____ IOUS
3. Fierce or savage (9) _____ IOUS
4. Very tasty or good to eat (9) _____ IOUS
5. Inquisitive (7) _____ IOUS
6. Successful in a battle or contest (10) _____ IOUS
7. Likely to hurt you and not safe (9) _____ OUS
8. Very large or excellent (10) _____ OUS
9. If you aim high and really want to achieve you are (9) _____ IOUS
10. To be careful or wary is to be (8) _____ IOUS

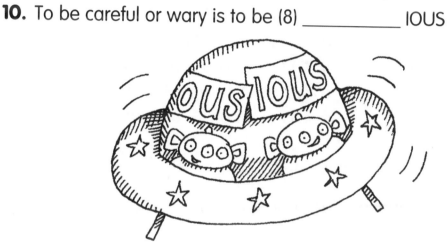

These words with **OUS** and **IOUS** have been split in two. Join the pieces to make a full word.

1. MIS   ICROUS   _____
2. LUD   TIOUS   _____
3. OBNOX   CHIEVOUS   _____
4. FICTI   IOUS   _____
5. CAUT   IOUS   _____
6. RELIG   OLOUS   _____
7. NUTRI   ERIOUS   _____
8. MYST   TROUS   _____
9. MONS   TIOUS   _____
10. FRIV   IOUS   _____

63

Words with OU and OUGH

OU and OUGH can be tricky as they can be pronounced in several different ways. There are no clear rules to help with pronunciation, so these need to be learnt and remembered.

The **OU** letter string has the following possible phonemes:

- **OW** as in *cow – cloud*;
- **U** as in *bus – nervous*;
- **OO** as in *loop – soup*;
- **O** as in *mole – mould*;
- **OR** as in *fort – court*.

The **OUGH** letter string has the following possible phonemes:

- **OW** as in *cow – bough*;
- **U** as in *gruff – rough*;
- **O** as in *no – dough*;
- **OO** as in *too – through*;
- **AU** as in *taught – bought*;
- **OU** as in *out – drought*.

Sort these **OU** words into rhyming groups in the table below.

~~pouch~~   sour   flounce   ground   mouse   hour
four   announce   slouch   louse   sound   your

OUR	POUR	ROUND	HOUSE	BOUNCE	OUCH
					pouch

Read the clues and unjumble the anagrams in brackets to make **OUGH** words.

1. A farming tool. (HOGULP)
2. A long container for animals' food or water. (HUGROT)
3. Careful, methodical or complete. (GHOTHROU)
4. The past tense of buy. (TUGHOB)
5. The past tense of bring. (ROBTHUG)

Words with CK

CK is often found at the end of words and sometimes in the middle. It always goes after a short vowel phoneme, for example, *duck*, *lick*, *cracked* and *pocket*. CK should not be confused with K + 'silent E' as these words are pronounced differently, for example, *snack – snake* and *back – bake*.

Read the clues compete this crossword. Use the word bank to help you.

Word bank

ROCKS	TRICKY	TICK	BRICK	CLOCK	SHIPWRECK	CRICKET	SHOCKING
JACKET	SPECK	STRUCK	RACKET	TRACK	NECKLACE	DECK	PECK
BUCKLE	KNUCKLE	QUACK	DUCK	STICK	LUCKY	CHUCKLING	SUCK

ACROSS

1. Stones or small boulders (5)   **3.** Difficult or complicated (6)   **7.** Laughing quietly or softly (9)   **8.** This has numbers, a face and hands (5)   **10.** A game played with a ball, bats and wickets (7)   **14.** The past tense of strike (6)   **16.** Jewellery worn around the throat (8)   **19.** A bird that goes quack (4)   **20.** A bony finger joint (7)
21. To join together with glue (5)   **22.** A path or rough road (5)

DOWN

2. A sunken ship (9)   **3.** The noise a clock makes '_ _ _ _ tock (4)   **4.** A block of hardened clay used for building (5)   **5.** Disgusting or astonishing (8)   **6.** A short coat (6)   **9.** A fastening on a belt or strap (6)   **11.** The sound made by a duck (5)
12. The floor of a ship or bus (4)   **13.** A short sharp bite with a beak (4)   **14.** A small spot or particle (5)   **15.** A loud noise or din (6)   **17.** Fortunate, for example, in games of chance (5)   **18.** You do this when you drink with a straw (4)

Words with K

The phonemes **K**, **C** and **CK** have the same sound, so it is important to know which letters to use. Use the rules below to help you decide and spell words correctly.

- **K** at the start of a word is usually followed by **I** or **E**, for example, *ki*ck and *ke*rb.
- When **K** is followed by **A** or **O**, the words often come from other countries, for example, *kangaroo*, *karate* and *koala*.
- A **hard C** phoneme never goes before **I** or **E**, as these vowels make the **C** soft, for example, *circle* and *certain*.
- The only words that end in **K** (without a **C**) are those with long vowel phonemes, for example, *leak*, *peek* and *soak*.
- **K** is often found with long vowels phonemes and 'silent **E**', for example, *snake*, *bike*, *poke* and *duke*.
- **K** can also be a silent letter combined with **N**, for example, *knife* and *knot*.

Unjumble these anagrams to make frequently used words that begin with **K**. In some, the **K** is silent.

1. PEKE _____

2. LKENNE _____

3. LETKET _____

4. SKEY _____

5. KIDECK _____

6. DINK _____

7. ILLKING _____

8. NECKTHI _____

9. SNEEK _____

10. GINK _____

11. KWON _____

12. TIKE _____

Words with K

Write the missing phoneme, **C** or **K**, in the following words.

1. __ ingfisher
2. __ amera
3. __ orrect
4. __ ountry
5. __ eyboard
6. __ rash
7. __ urious
8. __ indness
9. __ aptain
10. __ alendar
11. __ areful
12. __ ollect
13. __ ompass
14. __ ilogram
15. __ ilometre
16. __ upboard
17. __ rystal
18. __ lever
19. __ nuckle
20. __ nowledge

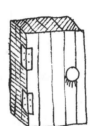

Find and circle the 12 words with **K** in this letter puzzle. The first one has been done for you.

ba ker year thqu ak eke elken nels mok espo ken
bro kenk news tri kek now led geke enk nock

Words with V

V is an interesting phoneme with some important rules for how to use it.

- There are no words in English that end in **V**. The **V** is always followed by **E**, for example, *give* and *have*.
- There are also no words with a double **V**.
- The letter string **UV** is not found in English so this is spelt **OVE**, for example, *love* and *dove*.
- In plural nouns **V** often replaces **F**, for example, *knife* – *kniv**es***.

Write the words beside the clues in lower case letters. Then, fill in the missing letters in the word wall in upper case letters.

1. An antonym for hate _____
2. A white bird, similar to a pigeon _____
3. To find something _____
4. You wear these on your hands _____
5. An antonym for below _____
6. To push hard _____
7. To stay in one place in the air _____
8. A stove or cooker _____
9. A fictional book _____
10. A type of spade used to move sand, snow or coal _____

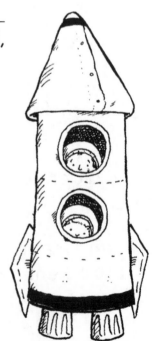

Words with V

Find and circle the 12 words with **V** in this letter puzzle. The first one has been done for you.

ri ver del ive rqui verli vingcar ni valsh iv ergi venunco ver
sta rvema rvel louss ilve rm ove

Write the singular form of the following plural nouns with **V**.

1. scarves _____
2. knives _____
3. loaves _____
4. shelves _____
5. elves _____
6. wolves _____

Say the words below and sort them into two groups using the table, according to their vowel phonemes. Two words have been written in for you.

give survive drive shiver diver wives deliver hive
active snivel gravel grave wave have massive olive
grove over cover hover clover even every stove

Short vowel phonemes		Long vowel phonemes	
give		hive	

Words with **SS**

SS is often found at the end of words and sometimes in the middle. It always follows a short vowel phoneme, for example, *floss*, *message* and *crossing*. It is sometimes spelt with one **S**, for example, *plus*, *minus*, *gas* and *thesaurus*, but often a single **S** sounds more like **Z**, for example, *is*, *his*, *as* and *was*.

Find and circle the 12 **SS** words in this letter puzzle. The first one has been done for you.

(wait ress)prin ces scro sse xpressi onper missi onp res sure

clas sad dres shis slo sshap pines spas sing

Write the missing **SS** words in these sentences.

 PRESSED   LESS   DISCUSS   WAITRESSES   MOSS   CROSSINGS
DRESS   TRESPASSING   FEARLESS   GUESS   CHESS   MESSY
GLOSS   MISS   MISSING

1. The sign on the big gate said 'Private No _____'.
2. I didn't know the answer, so I had to _____.
3. We decided to use shiny _____ paint not matt.
4. The brave soldiers were strong and _____.
5. Before a woman gets married, her title is _____, not Mrs.
6. _____ is a board game with knights, kings, queens, bishops and pawns.
7. My writing was so _____ I had to do it again neatly.
8. The fishermen were still _____ so the coastguards carried on searching.
9. Pedestrian _____ are there to help people get across the road safely.
10. A ballgown is a type of _____ for formal dancing.
11. Down by the stream, the rocks were damp and covered in _____.
12. The man was disappointed, because instead of getting more money, he got _____.
13. We all got together to _____ what to do next.
14. The restaurant was very busy and there were lots of waiters and _____ working there.
15. I _____ my best clothes very carefully with the iron.

Words that end in FF and LL

The words in these puzzles end in **FF** or **LL** and they usually have short vowel phonemes: *cuff* and *will*. There are exceptions to this rule:
- **ALL**, for example, *ball* (the odd word out is *shall*).
  - **ULL**, for example, *dull* and *pull*.

Complete the words in the flying saucers by writing in the missing letters. The words underneath each other all rhyme and end in **LL**. The clues are not in the right order but they will help you work out the answers.

A sudden strong wind.
To excite suddenly.
Everyone or everything.
Not moving.
An antonym for big.
Sick or unwell.
To shout or cry out.
An invoice or a bird's beak.

★ ★

A deep hole dug for water.
The main part of a boat.
This makes a ringing sound.
The bones of your head.
The hard cover round a nut or egg.
A sea bird.

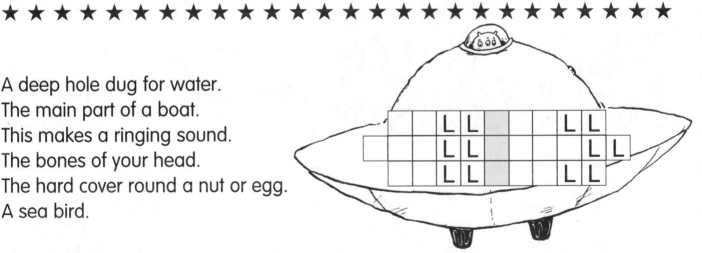

Choose the correct vowel (**A, E, I, O,** or **U**) for the following words that end in **FF** and complete the words on the lines.

1. SN_____   **2.** WH_____   **3.** SCR_____   **4.** DANDR_____

5. P_____   **6.** SHER_____   **7.** C_____

Words with WA

W is an unusual consonant, as when it appears before **A** it can change the sound of the phoneme:
- before a short **A** it sounds like a short **O** and **OR**, for example, *was* and *warn*.

Write the words with **WA** in this crossword.

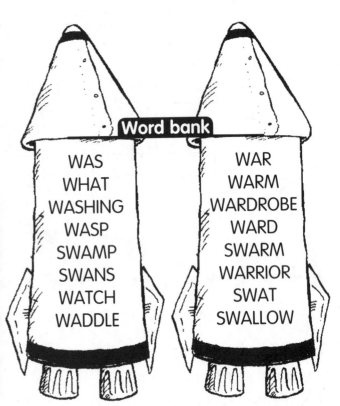

Word bank

WAS
WHAT
WASHING
WASP
SWAMP
SWANS
WATCH
WADDLE

WAR
WARM
WARDROBE
WARD
SWARM
WARRIOR
SWAT
SWALLOW

ACROSS
1. To walk like a duck (6) **2.** A small clock you can wear on your wrist (5) **4.** To hit or crush a fly (4) **6.** A stinging insect (4) **7.** White, long necked water birds (5) **8.** You can hang your clothes in this (8) **9.** An antonym for peace (3) **10.** Cleaning clothes or hands (7) **11.** A room in a hospital for patients (4)

DOWN
1. An impolite way of saying 'pardon' (4) **3.** A large number of bees (5) **4.** To make something go down your throat (7) **5.** Fairly hot (4) **7.** A marshy area (5) **8.** Someone who fights in battles, a soldier (7) **11.** The past tense of is (3)

Words with WO

W is an unusual consonant, as when it appears before **O** it can change the sound of the phoneme:
- before **O**, it sounds like a short **U**, for example, *worry* and *wonder*;
- before **OR**, it sounds like **ER**, for example, *word* and *work*.

Write the answers beside the clues in lower case letters. All the words contain **WO**. Then find the answers in the wordsearch.

1. Letters are needed to spell these (5) _____

2. An antonym for play (4) _____

3. The earth with all its countries and people (5) _____

4. An antonym for better (5) _____

5. Marvellous and amazing (9) _____

6. An antonym for best (5) _____

7. To be anxious or concerned is to (5) _____

8. A long thin creature that wriggles through the soil (4) _____

9. An antonym for lost (5) _____

10. A place where things are made or mended (8) _____

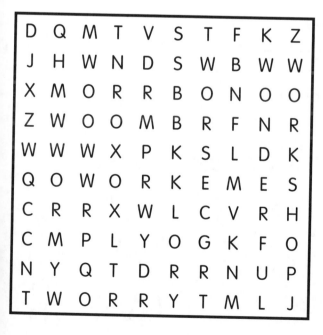

D	Q	M	T	V	S	T	F	K	Z
J	H	W	N	D	S	W	B	W	W
X	M	O	R	R	B	O	N	O	O
Z	W	O	O	M	B	R	F	N	R
W	W	W	X	P	K	S	L	D	K
Q	O	W	O	R	K	E	M	E	S
C	R	R	X	W	L	C	V	R	H
C	M	P	L	Y	O	G	K	F	O
N	Y	Q	T	D	R	R	N	U	P
T	W	O	R	R	Y	T	M	L	J

Word bank

WORKSHOP
WORRY
WORK
WORLD
WORSE
WORDS
WONDERFUL
WORST
WORM
WON

Words with similar patterns and meanings

There are many words in the English language with similar patterns and meanings. Sometimes we find words within compound words, for example, *overtime, timetable, upset, upright* and *handbag*. Sometimes we can hear letter strings that have the same meaning, for example, *medicine, medicate* and *medical*. Listening for these patterns and meanings can help you spell words correctly.

★ ★

Find and circle the seven compound words with **OUT** in this letter puzzle. The first one has been done for you.

wit hout o uts ideo utli neloo kouto utla wth rough ou tout doors

Find and circle the seven compound words with **OVER** in this letter puzzle.

o verh ead tur nove rover grow nover dueo verf low walko vero verb oard

These words all begin with **FOR**. Read the clues and write in the complete words on the lines.
1. An antonym for remember _____
2. To stop being angry with someone after they say sorry _____
3. An antonym for backwards _____
4. An antonym for giving permission _____
5. A synonym for luckily _____

These words all contain **ROOM**. Read the clues and write in the complete words on the lines.
1. A room where you sleep _____
2. A room where you eat meals _____
3. Spacious and not cramped _____
4. Someone who shares a room with someone else _____ - _____
5. A room where you wait _____

Unjumble the following anagrams to make words with **LIGHT**.

1. LINGTHING _____
2. SHOUTHIGLE _____
3. PLOTSTHIG _____
4. THERGIL _____
5. GLIDETH _____

Words with similar patterns and meanings

These words can become compound words by adding **WATER**. Read the clues, choose which word belongs to each clue and write the complete compound words on the lines.

★ LOGGED FALL PROOF TIGHT UNDER ★

1. A coat that keeps you dry in the rain is _____
2. A container that doesn't let water spill out is _____
3. Something that is soaked or filled with water is _____
4. A stream or river of water falling from a high place is a _____
5. A diver with an oxygen tank can swim _____

Under or over? These words have the prefixes **UNDER** or **OVER**. Read the clues and add the correct prefix to the words.

1. Protective work clothing – _____alls
2. When the sky is covered with cloud – _____cast
3. Below the earth's surface – _____ground
4. A kind of bridge – _____pass
5. To take too much medicine – _____dose
6. Secret or deceitful – _____hand
7. To wake up later than planned – _____sleep
8. Covered with weeds or wild plants – _____grown
9. On the ground that you walk on – _____foot
10. To pass another moving car or person – _____take
11. Clothes worn next to the skin – _____wear
12. A subway – _____pass
13. Floor covering beneath a carpet – _____lay
14. Below something – _____neath

Words with the prefixes UN, MIS, NON and DIS

The prefixes **UN**, **MIS**, **NON** and **DIS** can be added to words to make them mean the opposite, for example, *happy – **un**happy, understand – **mis**understand, sense – **non**sense* and *pleased – **dis**pleased*. In some cases the root word is less obvious or is no longer used on its own, for example, *uncanny, mistake, nondescript* and *disappointed*. **UN** is the most commonly used of this group and **NON** is often followed by a hyphen, for example, *non – existent*.

Read the clues and add the prefixes **UN**, **MIS**, **NON** or **DIS** to complete the words.

1. Bad luck – _____fortune
2. Not easily caught on fire – _____flammable
3. Not truthful – _____ honest
4. Not able to make up your mind – _____decided
5. Out of work – _____employed
6. Rare and not often seen – _____common
7. To be naughty – _____behave
8. A type of book that has facts not stories – _____fiction
9. To vanish from sight – _____appear
10. Not very probable – _____likely

Choose the correct prefixes for the following words and write the new words in the table. The first has been done for you.

UN or DIS	DIS or MIS	MIS or NON	UN or NON
*un*comfortable	like	trust	certain
graceful	treat	renewable	stick
agree	understood	fit	believable
healthy	order	existent	cover
popular	miss	lead	stop

Prefixes revision

The following words contain a variety of prefixes: **A, AL, ANTI, BE, CO, DE, DIS, EX, IN, MIS, NON, PRE, RE, UN** and **TO**.

The prefix for each answer is given (in brackets) at the end of each clue. Complete the clues, then fill in the answers in this crossword.

ACROSS

4. The doctor used an _____ cream on my cut, to stop any infection (ANTI) (10)   **5.** The circus performer walked _____ the tight rope, to the other side of the big top (A) (5)   **9.** People get on much better when they _____ and work together (CO) (9)   **11.** The toddler was talking _____ and it didn't mean anything (NON) (8)   **16.** Dinosaurs lived ages ago in _____ times (PRE) (11)   **17.** A synonym for truthful (DIS) (9)

DOWN

1. An antonym for outside (IN) (6)   **2.** I had to buy a new book, to _____ the one that I damaged (RE) (7)   **3.** This policeman looks for clues and evidence (DE) (9)   **6.** Another word for confused, puzzled and worried (BE) (10)   **7.** The things that you own are your _____ (BE) (10)   **8.** To fool someone by lying, is to _____ them (DE) (7)   **10.** An error is another word for a _____ (MIS) (7)   **12.** My teacher's desk is very _____, but she knows where everything is (UN) (6)   **13.** The bus had _____ left when we got there, so we missed it (AL) (7)   **14.** Some animals are now _____ (EX) (7)   **15.** Rare and not often seen (UN) (8)

Compound words

Compound words are made up of two or smaller words joined together to make one long word, for example, *bedroom*, *eyesight* and *hairbrush*. Another type of compound word can be made when prefixes or suffixes are added to words, for example, *hopeless*, *hopeful*, *unhappy*, *undress* and *unaware*.

1st word	2nd word	Complete word
sauce	bow	saucepan
home	noon	
rain	fast	
after	print	
break	doors	
every	post	
paper	table	
sign	copy	
foot	quake	
time	where	
earth	work	
photo	back	
in	pan	

The table of compound words have been muddled up. Join together the correct words (in the two columns) to make longer compound words and write them in the empty column. One has been done for you.

Add a second word to the words below to make compound words.

1. LIGHT _____
2. SNOW _____
3. WEEK _____
4. FIRE _____
5. BATH _____
6. ANY _____

★★★ Add a first word to the words below to make compound words.

★ 1. _____ LACE
★ 2. _____ SICK
★ 3. _____ ROOM
★ 4. _____ WORD
★ 5. _____ PAPER
★ 6. _____ BODY

Compound words

Read the clues and unjumble the anagrams to make compound words. Each of the words within the compound word has a separate anagram, for example, *tew situ = wet suit = wetsuit*.

	Clue	Anagram	Compound word
1.	This is wet and drops straight down	twear	lalf _____
2.	All the people	ryvee	noe _____
3.	Not the ground floor	pu	tassir _____
4.	An antonym for hello	dogo	yeb _____
5.	Not above the surface of the earth	duner	rogdun _____
6.	People send these when they are on holiday	stop	dracs _____
7.	The fringes of hair above the eyes	yee	worbs _____
8.	The place you go to catch a plane	ria	trop _____
9.	These can hold pieces of paper together	preap	plics _____
10.	Put this on a brush to clean your teeth	thoot	stape _____
11.	A very large golden flower	nus	rewolf _____
12.	Time to have a midday meal	chuln	mite _____

Now write a sentence for each of the compound words on a separate piece of paper.

Suffixes revision

SUFFIXES REVISION

The following words contain a variety of suffixes: **ABLE, AL, ARY, ATE, ED, ETTE, FUL, HOOD, IBLE, IC, IFY, IOUS, ING, IST, SHIP, MENT, FUL, LIKE, LY, NESS, OUS, SION, TION** and **WORTHY**. The suffix for each answer is given (in brackets) at the end of each clue. Complete the sentences.

1. Not able to be broken (**ABLE**) _____

2. The final practice of a play is called a dress (**AL**) _____

3. A yearly celebration of an important date (**ARY**) _____

4. To change words from one language to another (**ATE**) _____

5. An antonym for answered (**ED**) _____

6. A shop where clothes can be washed in coin operated machines (**ETTE**) _____

7. Cautious (**FUL**) _____

8. During your _____ years you usually go to school (**HOOD**)

9. Unbelievable and amazing (**IBLE**) _____

10. Creative and good at drawing and painting (**IC**) _____

11. To rule someone out of a race or competition for breaking the rules (**IFY**) _____

12. This type of disease can be passed on from person to person (**IOUS**) _____

13. An antonym for coming (**ING**) _____

14. Someone who writes for a newspaper (**IST**) _____

15. People with _____ skills are able to direct and manage others (**SHIP**)

16. Gear, apparatus or tools (**MENT**) _____

17. Sore and hurting (**FUL**) _____

18. A _____ woman is polite and refined (**LIKE**)

19. An antonym for quickly (**LY**) _____

20. In the evening the sun sets and _____ falls (**NESS**)

21. Huge or vast (**OUS**) _____

22. An antonym for multiplication (**SION**) _____

23. A group of things gathered together is a _____ (**TION**)

24. A car can only be driven safely if it is _____ (**WORTHY**)

Suffixes revision

The following words contain a variety of suffixes: **ABLE, AL, ARY, ATE, ED, ETTE, FUL, HOOD, IBLE, IC, IFY, IOUS, ING, IST, SHIP, MENT, FUL, LIKE, LY, NESS, OUS, SION, TION** and **WORTHY.** Highlight the words from the word bank in the wordsearch.

Word bank

REHEARSAL	COLLECTION	CHILDHOOD	GOING
ANNIVERSARY	CAREFUL	ARTISTIC	JOURNALIST
LAUNDRETTE	LADYLIKE	SLOWLY	DISQUALIFY
UNBREAKABLE	EQUIPMENT	ROADWORTHY	LEADERSHIP
TRANSLATE	PAINFUL	DIVISION	DARKNESS
ASKED	INCREDIBLE	INFECTIOUS	ENORMOUS

```
D C A T L D Q J O U R N A L I S T Q R N
Y I B N P C A K M F R K A R T I S T I C
B X S K N A A R T P M H E N O R M O U S
H L K Q N I I R K J D Z V T K R T L C M
T Q C M U G V N E N P Z P P T R W V L M
K N H K D A M E F F E N P N K W D H G Z
W T I V I L L J R U U S L V T W P P X W
H H L T V Q M I L S L L S W X L N N N K
L I D R I B L F F Y A R E H E A R S A L
A N H A S G D K L Y Y R E L Y K L R R P
D F O N I B M W G H E L Y B N D G G H N
Y E O S O P O C T L B D D O Z N X F G M
L C D L N L C R B A E B I L I K N Q M N
I T Z A S W O I K K M T Q O Y D M C K Q
K I D T W W D A S D C X G G R M T T F L
E O M E D E E A F E R H B N T G T N N N
H U Y A R R R Z L L E A D E R S H I P L
Y S O C B Z J L V E Q U I P M E N T K T
G R N N R X O X R J X M Q R Y M K N L G
N I U K N C J L A U N D R E T T E K C R
```

Commonly misspelt words

The words on this page are difficult to spell correctly, but if you practise using them you will be able to get them right.

Some words can be shortened with the use of an apostrophe, for example, *cannot – can't*. Remember that the apostrophe takes the place of the missing letter or letters. However, *will not* is unusual as it is shortened to become *won't*.

Write the shortened words in this table.

	Complete words	Contraction		Complete words	Contraction
1.	I will		**7.**	was not	
2.	shall not		**8.**	they are	
3.	did not		**9.**	we are	
4.	could not		**10.**	had not	
5.	do not		**11.**	has not	
6.	were not		**12.**	have not	

1. mother   muther _____

2. bruther   brother _____

3. neice   niece _____

4. uncle   unkle _____

5. neffew   nephew _____

6. farther   father _____

7. arent   aunt _____

8. sister   sitser _____

9. granfather   grandfather _____

10. granmother   grandmother _____

Choose the correct spelling for these different family members and write them on the lines.

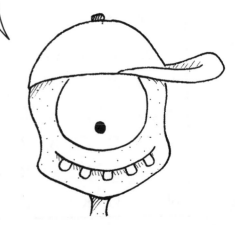

Commonly misspelt words

The answers to the clues are all words that are often spelt incorrectly.

ACROSS

3. This is measured in kilograms and grams (6)   **6.** A companion or buddy (6)
7. All the people (8)   **10.** An impolite way of saying 'pardon' when you don't hear someone clearly (4)   **13.** An antonym for back (5)   **14.** You use your ears to do this (6)
16. Buying things (8)   **17.** A measurement of how tall something is (6)   **20.** The day before Sunday (8)   **21.** To feel sure that something is true (7)   **22.** The day after Tuesday (9)

DOWN

1. For sure or certainly (10)   **2.** A seat belt in a car is sometimes called a _____ belt (6)   **4.** I was _____ a lovely time at the beach (6)   **5.** An antonym for ugly (9)   **8.** The plural of baby (6)   **9.** You can write on this (5)   **10.** Which person? (3)   **11.** We wear these (7)   **12.** For the reason that (7)   **15.** A flat crisp cake also called a cookie (7)   **18.** Another word for a vacation (7)   **19.** Frightened (6)
20. The past tense of say (4)

Answers

■ PAGE 6

Verb – present tense	Verb – past tense	Verb – present tense	Verb – past tense
ASK	ASKED	OPEN	OPENED
BEGIN	BEGAN	SHOW	SHOWED
HEAR	HEARD	THINK	THOUGHT
KNOW	KNEW	WATCH	WATCHED
BRING	BROUGHT	WAKE	WOKE
WRITE	WROTE	USE	USED
START	STARTED	LEAVE	LEFT
FIND	FOUND	TURN	TURNED
CHANGE	CHANGED	TELL	TOLD
JUMP	JUMPED	WALK	WALKED

1. ANY
2. BEING
3. CHANGE
4. DOES
5. DON'T
6. EVERY
7. GONE
8. MIGHT
9. MUCH
10. NEVER
11. NUMBER
12. ONLY
13. PLACE
14. STILL
15. TOLD
16. TRIES
17. UPON
18. WHERE
19. WHILE
20. WITHOUT

■ PAGE 7

■ PAGE 8

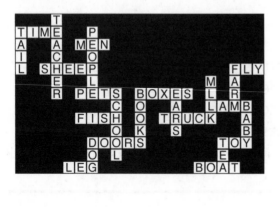

■ PAGE 9

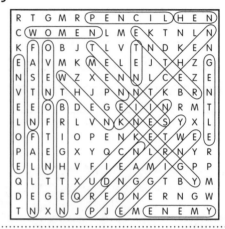

chicken general enjoy then tent spend plenty generous

■ PAGE 10

1 syllable	2 syllables	3 syllables
ran	planets	manager
Nan	woman	caravan
man	human	animals
fan	began	anagram
Dan		Canada
can		banana
plan		
flan		
van		
tan		

■ PAGE 11

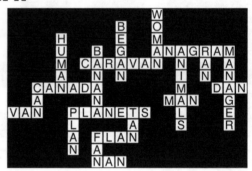

■ PAGE 12

1. chapter
2. cap
3. collapse
4. wrap
5. chap
6. capsized
7. sap
8. captain
9. strap
10. map
11. happy
12. evaporate
13. Japan
14. tap
15. nap
16. gap
17. yap

18. trap
19. capital
20. kidnap
21. flap
22. apple

■ PAGE 13

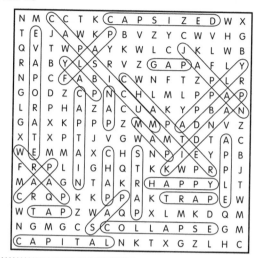

1. APPLE
2. APPLY
3. CAP
4. CAPITAL
5. CAPSICUM
6. CAPSIZED
7. CAPTAIN
8. CHAP
9. CHAPTER
10. COLLAPSE
11. EVAPORATE
12. FLAP
13. GAP
14. HAPPY
15. JAPAN
16. KIDNAP
17. MAP
18. NAP
19. SAP
20. STRAP
21. TAP
22. TRAP
23. WRAP
24. YAP

■ PAGE 14

1. SATELLITE
2. CATAPULT
3. THAT
4. FLAT
5. CATERPILLAR
6. SATURN
7. BATON
8. WOMBAT
9. ATLAS
10. SATURDAY

■ PAGE 15

1 syllable	2 syllables	3 syllables	4 syllables
sat	baton	atmosphere	catamaran
rat	atlas	satisfied	material
mat	flatten	gratitude	category
that	batter	acrobat	fanatical
brat	satin	catapult	catastrophic
gnat	format	habitat	diplomatic

atlas   mattress   format   combat

automatic   democratic   latitude   flattery

■ PAGE 16

1. My older brother loves to play **CRICKET** and he is a great bowler.
2. The soldiers stopped firing when they ran out of **BULLETS**.
3. It was so cold I needed an extra **BLANKET** on my bed.
4. I have a silver **LOCKET** with a picture of my grandmother inside it.
5. I went to town and **MET** my best friend to go shopping.
6. My dad wears a leather **JACKET** when he rides his motorbike.
7. There are 26 letters in the **ALPHABET**.
8. My teacher hates it when we **FIDGET** and she tells us to sit still.

A	E	I	O	U
BASKET	FERRET	MILLET	SOCKET	BUCKET
PACKET	HELMET	FILLET	LOCKET	CRUMPET
PLANET	PELMET	CRICKET	ROCKET	TURRET
MAGNET	VELVET	WICKET	BONNET	JUNKET
GADGET	PELLET	INLET	GOBLET	BUDGET

■ PAGE 17

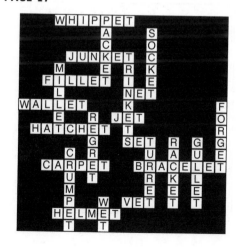

■ **PAGE 18**

■ **PAGE 19**

1 syllable	2 syllables	3 syllables
TWIG	WRIGGLE	VIGOROUS
WIG	TRIGGER	CIGARETTES
RIG	SNIGGER	SIGNATURE
PIG	RIGGING	IGNORANT
DIG	ZIGZAG	IGUANA
	SIGNAL	
	PIGLET	
	JIGSAW	
	IGNORE	
	IGNITE	
	GIGGLE	
	FIGURE	

■ **PAGE 20**

1. winter
2. fascinating
3. bin
4. thin
5. opinions
6. grin
7. begin
8. finish
9. chin
10. original

Noun – singular	Noun – plural	Verb	Adjective
GRIN	OPINIONS	GRIN	FASCINATING
BIN		BIN	ORIGINAL
CHIN		BEGIN	THIN
WINTER		FINISH	
FINISH			

■ **PAGE 21**

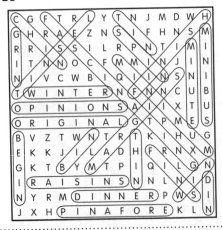

1. minute
2. win
3. tinsel
4. minibus
5. raisins
6. spin
7. tin
8. fins
9. dinner
10. margins
11. minimum
12. pinafore
13. din

■ **PAGE 22**

1. ship
2. tip
3. zip
4. chips
5. script
6. lipstick
7. slippers
8. flippers
9. rip
10. dip

■ **PAGE 23**

1. My new trousers were the right size around the waist, but too big on the **HIPS**.

2. The puppy kept **NIPPING** people and it had to be trained not to bite.

3. To make a meringue you have to **WHIP** the egg whites until they are stiff.

4. The nurse used a thin **STRIP** of material, in place of a bandage.

5. When I was learning to ride my bike, I used to **GRIP** the handlebars really tightly with my hands.

6. My dog licks his **LIPS** when he knows it's dinner time.

7. The leaky tap would not stop **DRIPPING**.

8. We went on a great **TRIP** to Europe in the holidays.

9. The drinks were so hot, we had to **SIP** them slowly.

10. It was so calm, there were only little **RIPPLES** on the water.

11. The **CLIPS** on the case were broken and it wouldn't close properly.

12. To turn a pancake over, if you are really clever, you can **FLIP** it up into the air.

■ PAGE 24

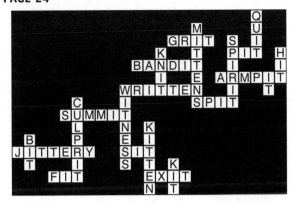

■ PAGE 25

helicopter hop gallop topic mopping crops topple hop optician top hopped chopping copy drop stop crops

1. DROPS
2. SLOPPY
3. CHOP
4. CLOP
5. OPERA
6. STOP
7. DEVELOP
8. POP
9. POPULAR

OP in 1st syllable	OP in 2nd syllable	OP in 3rd syllable
operation	wallop	helicopter
popcorn	scallop	develop
sloppy	gallop	lollipop
popper	raindrop	
dropping	workshop	
topic	backstop	
opera		

■ PAGE 26

1. carrot
2. apricot
3. dot
4. shot
5. robot
6. botany
7. got
8. rotten
9. ballot
10. knots
11. spotty
12. teapot
13. ingot

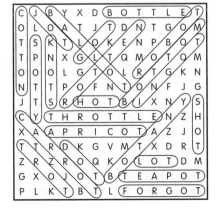

■ PAGE 27

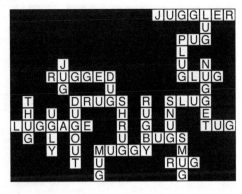

■ PAGE 28

under run jungle hundred punch stun uneasy bundle understand unhappy bunch funny junk dungeon puncture

Noun – singular	Noun – plural	Verb	Adjective
nun	dungarees	shun	uncanny
puncture	skunks	dunk	punctual
uncle	underpants	puncture	unhappy
bun	bunkbeds	underline	unfair
gun	chunks	munch	funny

■ PAGE 29

1. bunny
2. running
3. lunch
4. cunning
5. thunder
6. bunkbeds
7. punctual
8. underground
9. uneven
10. unfortunate

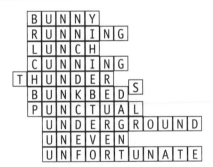

■ PAGE 30

sunflower   butterfly   replace   stapler   padlock
paddling   multiply   replay   unclear   sunglasses
toddler   overflow

1. Another word for an apartment is a **FLAT**.
2. To quickly run away from something is to **FLEE**.
3. The sharp hooked nails of animals are **CLAWS**.
4. The side of a hill or mountain is a **SLOPE**.
5. A **BLANKET** is a thick woollen bedcover.
6. **CLOCKS** help us to tell the time.
7. The coloured banners of countries are called **FLAGS**.
8. **CLUES** help you find answers to crosswords and crimes.
9. A plane that has no engine is a **GLIDER**.
10. A cut **BLEEDS** until the blood clots.
11. A group of sheep is called a **FLOCK**.
12. People who wear **GLASSES** have problems with their eyes.

■ PAGE 31

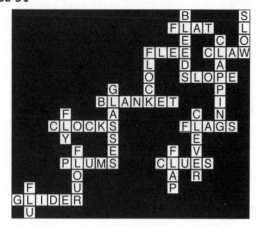

■ PAGE 32

1. TRAY
2. DRY
3. TREASURE
4. PRIZE
5. CREAM
6. BREAD
7. DREAM
8. TRACE
9. FRESH
10. BRIDGE
11. BRING
12. TRY
13. PRICE
14. FRY
15. FRIEND
16. FRAMES
17. FREEZE
18. CRY

■ PAGE 33

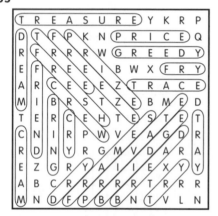

1. ATTRACTIVE
2. APRON
3. ACTRESS
4. ICECREAM
5. HAIRBRUSH
6. FINGERPRINTS
7. HUNDRED
8. MONGREL
9. AGREE
10. ELECTRICITY

■ PAGE 34

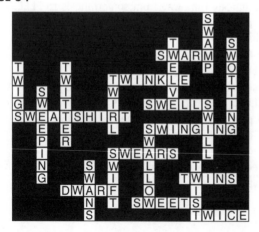

■ PAGE 35

1. SNEEZE
2. SPOONS
3. STIRRED
4. STAIRS
5. STARTED
6. SCARECROW
7. SNOWMAN
8. SQUARE
9. SNORING
10. SPOTTY
11. SQUEEZE
12. SKIRT
13. SKULL
14. SCARLET
15. SQUIRREL
16. SKYSCRAPER

1. WHISKERS
2. DISCUSS
3. CUSTARD
4. LOUDSPEAKER
5. TEASPOON
6. SISTER
7. ESCAPE
8. BASKET
9. ESKIMO
10. DISCOVER
11. CONSPIRACY
12. INSPECT
13. OUTSKIRTS
14. RESCUE
15. TRANSPORT

1. FANTASTIC
2. TELESCOPE
3. COSTUME
4. TRANSPARENT
5. DISMISS
6. SNAKE
7. SMOOTH
8. SPIDER
9. SQUASH
10. SMUGGLE

■ PAGE 36

1. BUTTERFLY
2. REPLY
3. STAPLER
4. WHISPER
5. SPIDERS
6. TABLESPOON
7. CROSSES
8. FROGS
9. STARS
10. NIGHTDRESS
11. CRATERS
12. COMPLAIN
13. LIBRARY
14. STAMPS
15. SCARF
16. CLOCK
17. DRY
18. DISASTER
19. DISQUALIFY
20. BLIND

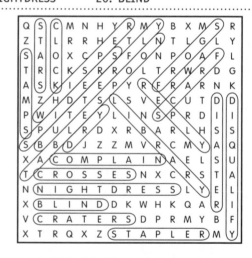

■ PAGE 37

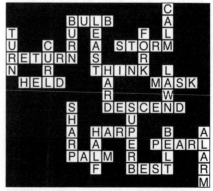

■ PAGE 38

1. M**AR**CH	9. CROSSW**OR**D
2. N**OR**TH	10. BIRD
3. PERSON	11. K**ER**B
4. THIRD	12. F**UR**RY
5. CHURCH	13. T**OR**CH
6. V**AR**NISH	14. F**ER**NS
7. M**AR**KET	15. F**AR**MER/F**OR**MER
8. W**OR**LD	16. SQUIRM

OR	CAR	SHIRK	CALM	CORN	CART
FOR	BAR	WORK	PALM	BORN	SMART
WAR	STAR	SMIRK	PSALM	WARN	TART
MORE	FAR	JERK		TORN	ART
CURB	**WORD**	**PORK**	**FARM**	**WORM**	**HURT**
KERB	HEARD	FORK	HARM	SQUIRM	BLURT
BLURB	BIRD	YORK	ALARM	FIRM	SHIRT
HERB	THIRD	CORK	CHARM	GERM	ALERT
CARD	**FIR**	**DARK**	**FERN**	**SHARP**	**SHORT**
HARD	HER	PARK	BURN	HARP	FORT
YARD	BLUR	ARK	TURN	CARP	EXPORT
LARD	STIR	LARK	LEARN		SNORT

■ PAGE 39

■ PAGE 40

1. TIGHT	8. WRITE
2. RIGHT	9. POLITE
3. BRIGHT	10. WHITE
4. FIGHT	11. KITE
5. LIGHT	12. DELIGHT
6. KNIGHT	13. STALACTITE
7. BITE	14. STALAGMITE

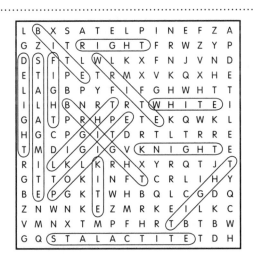

■ PAGE 41

1. Naked **bare**	A furry animal **bear**
2. A fruit **berry**	To put underground **bury**
3. To use your ears **hear**	Not there **here**
4. Not low **high**	An informal greeting **hi**
5. An antonym for war **peace**	A bit or part **piece**
6. An antonym for rich **poor**	To flow freely **pour**

1 To slow down and stop. **brake**
2 I **would** like to come, but I can't.
3 In the **past** people didn't have electricity.
4 During the **war** many soldiers were killed.
5 An amount, not exactly measured. **some**
6 This is often eaten for breakfast. **cereal**
7 I am going to **dye** my shirt red.
8 I have already **read** that book.
9 An elaborate chair for a king or queen. **throne**
10 The **tide** was in, so we could launch our boat.
11 My naughty puppy **chews** my slippers.

■ PAGE 42

cause   saucer   paws   draw   awful   automatic
claws   lawn

■ PAGE 43

1. SO**U**NDS	7. SOUTH
2. FLO**U**R	8. MO**U**THS
3. BR**OW**N	9. CLO**U**DS
4. DR**OW**N	10. ALL**OW**
5. V**OW**ELS	11. TR**OU**SERS
6. CR**OW**DED	12. H**OW**

1. B**OY**	9. P**OI**SON
2. S**OI**L	10. ENJ**OY**ABLE
3. ANN**OY**	11. **OI**NTMENT
4. DESTR**OY**	12. J**OI**NING
5. DISAPP**OI**NTED	13. C**OI**NS
6. P**OI**NT	14. APP**OI**NTMENT
7. V**OI**CE	15. CH**OI**CES
8. T**OI**LET	

■ PAGE 44

1. MAKE
2. GAME
3. AGAIN
4. PLAYTIME
5. SIXTEEN
6. STREETS
7. GREEN
8. FREEDOM

■ PAGE 45

1. WHITE
2. NIGHT
3. FLY
4. SMILE
5. TIPTOES
6. CLOSED
7. FOLLOW
8. BARBECUE
9. FUEL
10. NEPTUNE

■ PAGE 46

1. NIBBLE
2. BATTLE
3. BOTTLE
4. DRIBBLE
5. MIDDLE
6. NETTLE
7. THROTTLE
8. PUDDLES
9. RIDDLE

---

1. At the bowling alley we tried to knock down all the **SKITTLES**.

2. Worms like to **WRIGGLE** through the soil.

3. I was in such a **MUDDLE** I didn't know where to begin.

4. Another name for a violin is a **FIDDLE**.

5. The elderly man with the bad leg began to **HOBBLE** down the road.

6. My mum gives me a **CUDDLE** when I am feeling sad.

7. Men shave their faces to get rid of their **STUBBLE**.

8. The waves were so small they were only **RIPPLES**.

9. A crossword is a type of word **PUZZLE**.

■ PAGE 47

1. My brother had chicken pox and was very **SPOTTY**.

2. My big sister is really **BOSSY** and she is always telling me what to do.

3. At the fair we love to eat **TOFFEE** apples.

4. In the mornings, my mum loves a cup of **COFFEE**.

5. The gardener has to **SCATTER** the seeds evenly on the ground.

6. My favourite movies are **WESTERNS** with cowboys in them.

7. The farmer wanted to **FATTEN** the turkeys ready for Christmas.

8. I love chips with fish in crispy **BATTER**.

9. I was scared and excited when I went on the helter **SKELTER** at the fair.

10. When people meet they usually say hi, **HELLO** or a similar greeting.

11. When bananas turn from green to **YELLOW** you know they are ripe

12. The icing was too **RUNNY** and it slipped off the cake.

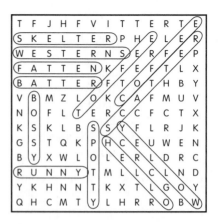

■ PAGE 48

Singular noun	Plural noun
key	keys
ghost	ghosts
lady	ladies
baby	babies
apple	apples
donkey	donkeys
fairy	fairies
story	stories
try	tries
orange	oranges
enemy	enemies
fly	flies
monkey	monkeys
television	televisions

■ PAGE 49

1. CHIMNEYS
2. TOYS
3. SPIES
4. BOYS
5. STRAYS
6. LOLLIES
7. DAYS
8. TRIES
9. FERRIES
10. BODIES
11. DISPLAYS
12. TRAYS

■ PAGE 50

Verb	Verb with S
carry	carries
play	plays
delay	delays
fry	fries
envy	envies
dry	dries
destroy	destroys
multiply	multiplies
disobey	disobeys
hurry	hurries

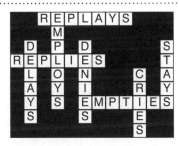

■ PAGE 51

■ PAGE 52

Verb	Verb with ING	Verb	Verb with ING
walk	walking	jump	jumping
whisk	whisking	earn	earning
punch	punching	twirl	twirling
own	owning	paint	painting
lick	licking	hiss	hissing
mess	messing	vanish	vanishing

Verb	Verb with ING	Verb	Verb with ING
whip	whipping	mop	mopping
drum	drumming	stab	stabbing
scrub	scrubbing	bob	bobbing
bug	bugging	skid	skidding
rip	ripping	flap	flapping
clip	clipped	knot	knotting

Verb	Verb with ING	Verb	Verb with ING
stay	staying	employ	employing
fly	flying	defy	defying
disobey	disobeying	obey	obeying
destroy	destroying	marry	marrying
worry	worrying	deny	denying
pry	prying	buy	buying

■ PAGE 53

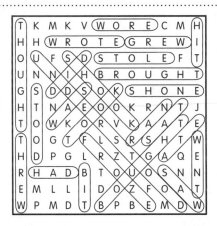

■ PAGE 54

Present tense	Past tense	Present tense	Past tense
have	had	understand	understood
am	was	wear	wore
go	went	run	ran
eat	ate	steal	stole
do	did	buy	bought
see	saw	bring	brought
think	thought	hit	hit
write	wrote	grow	grew
sit	sat	shake	shook
stand	stood	freeze	froze
shine	shone	bite	bit
take	took	throw	threw

■ PAGE 55

	Male	Female
1.	lion	lioness
2.	prince	princess
3.	actor	actress
4.	duke	duchess
5.	man	woman
6.	headmaster	headmistress

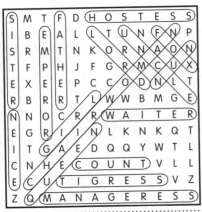

	Male	Female		Male	Female
1.	KING	QUEEN	9.	EMPEROR	EMPRESS
2.	COUNT	COUNTESS	10.	TIGER	TIGRESS
3.	LORD	LADY	11.	MONK	NUN
4.	NEPHEW	NEICE	12.	FOX	VIXEN
5.	CHAIRMAN	CHAIRWOMAN	13.	FATHER	MOTHER
6.	WAITER	WAITRESS	14.	BROTHER	SISTER
7.	HOST	HOSTESS	15.	BOY	GIRL
8.	UNCLE	AUNT	16.	MANAGER	MANAGERESS

■ **PAGE 56**

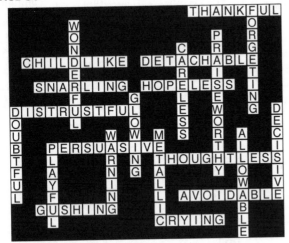

■ **PAGE 57**

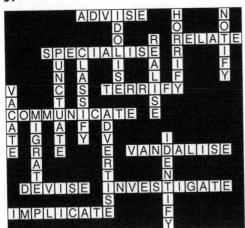

■ **PAGE 58**

1. rude**ness**
2. diction**ary**
3. sig**nal**
4. leader**ship**
5. athlet**ic**
6. champion**ship**
7. move**ment**
8. hero**ic**
9. amaze**ment**
10. child**hood**
11. moment**ary**
12. music**al**
13. brother**hood**
14. weak**ness**

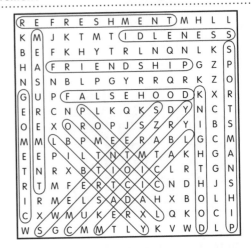

■ **PAGE 59**

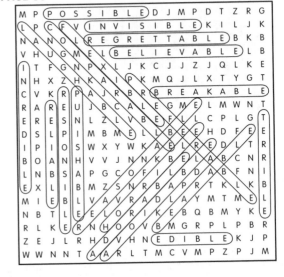

■ **PAGE 60**

■ PAGE 61

1. **al**most
2. **to**night
3. **al**together
4. **be**ware
5. **in**doors
6. **in**land
7. **al**ready
8. **to**day
9. **be**fore
10. **in**shore
11. **be**low
12. **a**part

■ PAGE 62

obnoxious   tedious   mischievous   marvellous
glorious   luxurious   mysterious

1. suspic**ious**
2. vigor**ous**
3. nerv**ous**
4. tremend**ous**
5. hilar**ious**
6. ob**v**ious
7. ridicul**ous**
8. fam**ous**
9. fur**ious**
10. prec**ious**

1. notorious
2. adventurous
3. superstitious
4. venomous
5. infectious
6. religious
7. ravenous
8. unconscious

■ PAGE 63

1. ENORMOUS
2. SERIOUS
3. FEROCIOUS
4. DELICIOUS
5. CURIOUS
6. VICTORIOUS
7. DANGEROUS
8. TREMENDOUS
9. AMBITIOUS
10. CAUTIOUS

1. MISCHIEVOUS
2. LUDICROUS
3. OBNOXIOUS
4. FICTITIOUS
5. CAUTIOUS
6. RELIGIOUS
7. NUTRITIOUS
8. MYSTERIOUS
9. MONSTROUS
10. FRIVOLOUS

■ PAGE 64

OUR	POUR	ROUND	HOUSE	BOUNCE	OUCH
sour	four	ground	mouse	flounce	pouch
hour	your	sound	louse	announce	slouch

1. PLOUGH
2. TROUGH
3. THOROUGH
4. BOUGHT
5. BROUGHT

■ PAGE 65

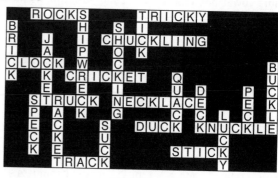

■ PAGE 66

1. KEEP
2. KENNEL
3. KETTLE
4. KEYS
5. KICKED
6. KIND
7. KILLING
8. KITCHEN
9. KNEES
10. KING
11. KNOW
12. KITE

■ PAGE 67

1. kingfisher
2. camera
3. correct
4. country
5. keyboard
6. crash
7. curious
8. kindness
9. captain
10. calendar
11. careful
12. collect
13. compass
14. kilogram
15. kilometre
16. cupboard
17. crystal
18. clever
19. knuckle
20. knowledge

bakery   earthquake   keel   kennel   smoke   spoken
broken   knew   strike   knowledge   keen   knock

■ PAGE 68

1. LOVE
2. DOVE
3. DISCOVER
4. GLOVES
5. ABOVE
6. SHOVE
7. HOVER
8. OVEN
9. NOVEL
10. SHOVEL

■ PAGE 69

river   deliver   quiver   living   carnival   shiver   given
uncover   starve   marvellous   silver   move

1. scarf
2. knife
3. loaf
4. shelf
5. elf
6. wolf

Short vowel phonemes		Long vowel phonemes	
give	shiver	hive	diver
deliver	active	survive	wives
snivel	gravel	drive	grave
have	massive	wave	clover
olive	cover	over	grove
hover	every	even	stove

■ PAGE 70

waitress   princess   cross   expression   permission
pressure   class   address   hiss   loss   happiness
passing

1. The sign on the big gate said 'Private No **TRESPASSING**'.
2. I didn't know the answer, so I had to **GUESS**.
3. We decided to use shiny **GLOSS** paint not matt.
4. The brave soldiers were strong and **FEARLESS**.
5. Before a woman gets married, her title is **MISS**, not Mrs.
6. **CHESS** is a great board game with knights, kings, queens, bishops and pawns.
7. My writing was so **MESSY** I had to do it again neatly.
8. The fishermen were still **MISSING** so the coastguards carried on searching.
9. Pedestrian **CROSSINGS** are there to help people get across the road safely.
10. A ballgown is a type of **DRESS** for formal dancing.
11. Down by the stream, the rocks were damp and covered in **MOSS**.
12. The man was disappointed, because instead of getting more money, he got **LESS**.
13. We all got together to **DISCUSS** what to do next.
14. The restaurant was very busy and there were lots of waiters and **WAITRESSES** working there.
15. I **PRESSED** my best clothes very carefully with the iron.

■ PAGE 71

A	L	L		I	L	L
C	A	L	L	B	I	L	L
S	M	A	L	L	S	T	I	L	L
S	Q	U	A	L	L	T	H	R	I	L	L

B	E	L	L		G	U	L	L
S	H	E	L	L	S	K	U	L	L
W	E	L	L	H	U	L	L

1. SNIFF or SNUFF
2. WHIFF
3. SCRUFF
4. DANDRUFF
5. PUFF
6. SHERIFF
7. CUFF

■ PAGE 72

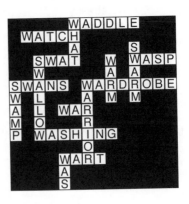

■ PAGE 73

1. WORDS
2. WORK
3. WORLD
4. WORSE
5. WONDERFUL
6. WORST
7. WORRY
8. WORM
9. WON
10. WORKSHOP

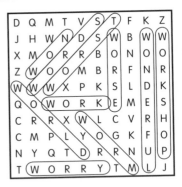

■ PAGE 74

without   outside   outline   lookout   outlaw   throughout
outdoors

overhead   turnover   overgrown   overdue   overflow
walkover   overboard

1. FORGET
2. FORGIVE
3. FORWARDS
4. FORBID
5. FORTUNATELY

1. BEDROOM
2. DINING ROOM
3. ROOMY
4. ROOM-MATE
5. WAITING ROOM

1. LIGHTNING
2. LIGHTHOUSE
3. SPOTLIGHT
4. LIGHTER
5. DELIGHT

■ **PAGE 75**

1. WATERPROOF
2. WATERTIGHT
3. WATERLOGGED
4. WATERFALL
5. UNDERWATER

1. **over**alls
2. **over**cast
3. **under**ground
4. **over**pass
5. **over**dose
6. **under**hand
7. **over**sleep
8. **over**grown
9. **under**foot
10. **over**take
11. **under**wear
12. **under**pass
13. **under**lay
14. **under**neath

■ **PAGE 76**

1. **mis**fortune
2. **non**-flammable
3. **dis**honest
4. **un**decided
5. **un**employed
6. **un**common
7. **mis**behave
8. **non**-fiction
9. **dis**appear
10. **un**likely

UN or DIS	DIS or MIS	MIS or NON	UN or NON
uncomfortable	**dis**like	**mis**trust	**un**certain
disgraceful	**mis**treat	**non**-renewable	**non**-stick
disagree	**mis**understood	**mis**fit	**un**believable
unhealthy	**dis**order	**non**-existent	**un**cover
unpopular	**dis**miss	**mis**lead	**non**-stop

■ **PAGE 77**

■ **PAGE 78**

Completed word
saucepan
homework
rainbow
afternoon
breakfast
everywhere
paperback
signpost
footprint
timetable
earthquake
photocopy
indoors

1. LIGHTHOUSE
2. SNOWBALL/MAN
3. WEEKEND/DAY
4. FIREMAN
5. BATHTUB/ROOM
6. ANYWHERE/BODY/THING

1. SHOELACE
2. SEA/HOMESICK
3. BED/BATH/DINING ROOM
4. CROSSWORD
5. NEWSPAPER
6. SOME/ANYBODY

■ **PAGE 79**

1. waterfall
2. everyone
3. upstairs
4. goodbye
5. underground
6. postcards
7. eyebrows
8. airport
9. paperclips
10. toothpaste
11. sunflower
12. lunchtime

■ **PAGE 80**

1. UNBREAKABLE
2. REHEARSAL
3. ANNIVERASARY
4. TRANSLATE
5. ASKED
6. LAUNDRETTE
7. CAREFUL
8. CHILDHOOD
9. INCREDIBLE
10. ARTISTIC
11. DISQUALIFY
12. INFECTIOUS
13. GOING
14. JOURNALIST
15. LEADERSHIP
16. EQUIPMENT
17. PAINFUL
18. LADYLIKE
19. SLOWLY
20. DARKNESS
21. ENORMOUS
22. DIVISION
23. COLLECTION
24. ROADWORTHY

■ **PAGE 81**

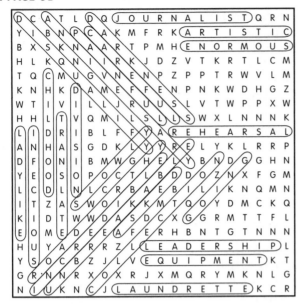

■ **PAGE 82**

	Complete words	Contraction
1.	I will	I'll
2.	shall not	shan't
3.	did not	didn't
4.	could not	couldn't
5.	do not	don't
6.	were not	weren't
7.	was not	wasn't
8.	they are	they're
9.	we are	we're
10.	had not	hadn't
11.	has not	hasn't
12.	have not	haven't

....

1. mother
2. brother
3. niece
4. uncle
5. nephew
6. father
7. aunt
8. sister
9. grandfather
10. grandmother

■ **PAGE 83**